Writing Abroad

A GUIDE FOR TRAVELERS

PETER CHILSON & JOANNE B. MULCAHY

The University of Chicago Press • Chicago and London

The University of Chicago Press, Chicago 60637
The University of Chicago Press, Ltd., London
© 2017 by Peter Chilson and Joanne B. Mulcahy
Published 2017
Printed in the United States of America

26 25 24 23 22 21 20 19 18 17 1 2 3 4 5

ISBN-13: 978-0-226-44435-2 (cloth)
ISBN-13: 978-0-226-44449-9 (paper)
ISBN-13: 978-0-226-44452-9 (e-book)
DOI: 10.7208/chicago/9780226444529.001.0001

Library of Congress Cataloging-in-Publication Data

Names: Chilson, Peter, author. | Mulcahy, Joanne B., 1954– author.
Title: Writing abroad : a guide for travelers / Peter Chilson and
Joanne B. Mulcahy.
Other titles: Chicago guides to writing, editing, and publishing.
Description: Chicago ; London : The University of Chicago Press, 2017. |
Series: Chicago guides to writing, editing, and publishing | Includes
bibliographical references and index.
Identifiers: LCCN 2017003729 | ISBN 9780226444352 (cloth : alk. paper) | ISBN
9780226444499 (pbk. : alk. paper) | ISBN 9780226444529 (e-book)
Subjects: LCSH: Travel writing—Handbooks, manuals, etc.
Classification: LCC G151 .C455 2017 | DDC 808.06/691—ddc23 LC record
available at https://lccn.loc.gov/2017003729

CONTENTS

INTRODUCTION

From Niger, West Africa, September 1986

In a motor park, a big open space where one can buy passage in a bus or a car, I was waiting for a minivan to a small village to visit a friend. An old man among the people waiting with me must have recognized something in my body language or on my face that betrayed my impatience. He put his hand on my shoulder and, offering me a toothless smile, said something in Hausa that I didn't understand. I smiled and looked at him quizzically. He was anxious for me to understand and asked a young man in the group to translate his words into French. "A patient man," the old man said, tapping the translator's shoulder, "can melt a rock." I nodded, embarrassed that I was so easy to read but impressed by the power and truth delivered in a proverb I could visualize. Here was a metaphor I had never heard and which expressed its meaning more effectively than simply saying, "Be patient!" The old man seemed to be asking me to take the time to understand something new.

PETER CHILSON, unpublished notebook

From Guanajuato, Mexico, January 2007

I was the only gringa on the bus from the city of Guanajuato to the nearby town of Valle de Santiago, the birthplace of my friend Eva Castellanoz. When I got off, a man in the station directed to me the local museum, for where else would a visitor want to go in this agricultural town? At the entrance, the curator, Marta Ruiz, greeted me. She stood about five foot two but would have been a few inches shorter without the heels. A broad smile filled her open, generous face. Red hair, a crimson sweater, and ruby fingernails enhanced her warmth. I asked Marta about legends Eva had told me that featured a monster inhabiting La Alberca, a nearby crater lake with mythic significance. Marta nodded. She'd heard stories about such a creature from her *abuelita* (grandmother). She mentioned Loch Ness as a point of reference for me. Where was he now, the monster? I asked, trying not to appear incredulous. She winked. "Gone north to Los Estados Unidos, looking for work, just like everyone else." We both burst out laughing but I wasn't sure who was the brunt of the joke.

JOANNE MULCAHY, unpublished notebook

These scenes recall lessons that we carried well beyond our time living in Niger and Mexico—moments that endured because we wrote about them. But writing doesn't just safeguard memories; the process can transform experience. All travel has an interior and exterior dimension. Writer Cynthia Ozick contrasts travel in which a "visitor passes through a place" with that in which "the place passes through" the person.[1] In writing, we capture both aspects of the journey—the wonders of places we pass through as well as the alchemy within us.

Daniel Boorstin distinguishes between travel and tourism, a distinction that's slippery but intriguing to consider. "There is," writes Boorstin, "a wonderful, but neglected, precision in these words."[2] "Travel" stems from "travail," signaling the hardships of mud-rutted roads, meager food, sickness at sea, and other painful experiences that characterized travel until the nineteenth century. Enter the "tourist," originally a hyphenated word, to characterize those who toured for pleasure. This shift, of course, also democratized travel. When

Thomas Cook began his rail excursions through England in the mid-nineteenth century, six hundred people joined the first group. The elite English who'd had exclusive access to travel balked at the thought of such a mob. John Ruskin wrote that being "sent" to a place was "very little different from becoming a parcel."[3] This tension between tourism and travel continues. "We are constantly being told," writes Peter Whitfield, "that true travel is now dead, killed by the age of mass tourism; but isn't this pure elitism?"[4] We sometimes struggle with the travail of travel while yearning for the comforts of tourism. Yet we keep going, hungry for learning about other people and places.

We intend this book for anyone who hopes to use writing and research to tell a story. Our goal is twofold: to help travelers deepen their understanding of another culture and to write about that new awareness in clear and vivid prose. Few intellectual exercises sharpen our minds as effectively as shaping thoughts into sentences. This is why new insights arise *as* we write. At every point, writing deepens our exploration of unknown terrain, new cultures and languages, and connections with people.

We have in mind travelers of all kinds: a student embarking on overseas study anywhere from Chile to Tajikistan; a retiree realizing a dream of seeing China; a software engineer in Russia on business; a Peace Corps worker in Kenya; a guide leading a trip to Portugal; a teacher of writing. But this book will also serve those discovering new regions of their own country. Keeping a journal would enhance the experience of northerners building houses with Habitat for Humanity in the rural South. As international educator Michael Woolf argues, "abroad" is not just a geographical designation. "Abroad" is a metaphor for what is less known, a journey across boundaries. These tools are adaptable to the needs of each person confronting the unfamiliar.

FREEWRITING THE JOURNEY

This book provides tools for writing at every stage of exploration: getting ready, being on-site in another culture, and returning to one's home country with new awareness. If writing is the medium, freewriting is the primary tool. Freewriting is writing without self-critique. We want to grope for knowledge, not state what we already know. The renowned writing teacher and theorist Peter Elbow says of freewriting: "The idea isn't to produce a polished piece of writing, but to simply get in the habit of writing without censoring and editing."[5] Travel writers, ethnographers, documentarians, and explorers of all kinds discipline themselves to write when they're tired, in the cold and wet, on whatever is at hand. The English writer Graham Greene wrote every day, five hundred words at a sitting, no matter where he was, often in a little notebook he carried. Poet Diane Thiel likens freewriting to "loosing a flood"—an appropriate metaphor for the barrage of images, sensations, sounds, tastes, and smells that assail us in a new culture. Each chapter in this book includes writing prompts and exercises to channel that flood into creative form; each integrates exemplary writing that achieves this goal. In the end, we're after stories— listening to those of others and fashioning our own to share with wider audiences. Facts are foundational, but stories connect us to the experiences of others. We recognize our shared humanity in the endless variety of cultures.

The experience of encountering a new culture shifts and gains depth each day. Peace Corps volunteers, for example, are trained to expect significant emotional highs and lows in their first months of service. An unfamiliar language, a different set of values, and the demands of a new job all present challenges. Often, mistakes and even humiliation guide learning. How do we decide how far to stand from someone on a bus or how much to eat at dinner? Should we kneel or bow as a guest at a religious ceremony, mimicking what others do, or observe from a distance? What blunders will we make in mastering an unfamiliar language? Without a record of those first false steps, we quickly forget how far we've come. Writing reveals the path to understanding as well as the distance covered. In all that trial and error, there might just be a good story to write.

RESEARCHING THE JOURNEY

A dedicated traveler records experience and does research at all stages of cultural exploration. As preparation, students or travelers should delve into libraries and websites, read online newspapers, explore the arts and film traditions of the region, and consult guidebooks, histories, and travel literature. Without prior knowledge of a place, it's easy to misinterpret or miss cultural cues. Onsite investigation will deepen understanding, especially as language mastery grows; on returning home, fact-checking and further revision will strengthen the writing.

The vast array of travel writing reflects the frailties and strengths of the observer as well as the assumptions of different historical periods. Reading insider and outsider perspectives creates important points of comparison. In chapter 1, we contrast the fourteenth-century Berber Muslim scholar and traveler Ibn Battuta's vision of Morocco with that of early twentieth-century American writer Edith Wharton. Travel literature might record life in one place as well as continuous journeys like Battuta's. In chapter 2, we note how African American writer James Baldwin focused his lens on mid-twentieth-century Paris.

Some travelers embark on the journey because they have the means and the curiosity. Some, like the Scottish doctor Mungo Park, are sanctioned by governments. He explored West Africa at the end of the eighteenth century on behalf of the British African Association, a club of wealthy men who sought to expand scientific knowledge and Britain's stake in world commerce. Others—refugees, war survivors—have no choice. Travel equals escape. Primo Levi's memoir, *The Truce*, tells the story of his slow journey home to Italy after liberation from Auschwitz, offering a startling eyewitness account of Europe in the first weeks and months after the end of World War II. Given this array of possibilities, we need to keep in mind what Peter Whitfield calls "the archetypal paradigm of travel"—"the conviction that travel is deeply purposeful: as we move through space, we are changed, we discover, and we are transformed."[6]

Research stretches beyond the library with "fieldwork," the term used by anthropologists, documentarians, folklorists, and others who delve into cultures as participant observers. Thoughtful travelers put aside their own cultural lenses and immerse themselves in the language, family life, literature, food, politics, commerce, fashion, and arts of a place. Taking part in cultural life, then stepping back to write about and interpret that experience, is the heart of participant observation.

Immersion journalists also rely on participant observation, spending anywhere from several weeks to a few years living in and writing about a culture. Immersion must involve critical reflection, an essential part of the writing process. This is particularly important for students studying abroad. As Michael Woolf reminds us, cultural immersion can be "closer to drowning than baptism." We can't assume that "mere proximity will bring enlightenment."[7]

DESIGNING THE JOURNEY: HOW THIS BOOK WORKS

Part One: Encountering Cultures

The Writer Abroad is divided into two overarching sections: "Encountering Cultures" and "Return and Revision." Within "Encountering Cultures," each of eight chapters details a different type of experience. We begin with the cultures we come from because these shape how we see the world and define "natural" behavior. We then move to encounters with new cultures; languages; portraits of people; landscape and setting; history, politics, and religion. We examine the relationship of writing to new technologies and social media, discussing the Internet, Skype, e-mail, Facebook, Twitter, and blogs. Chapter 4 gives an overview of documentary media and methods that complement writing—oral history interviews, film, photography, digital stories, and other forms.

In each chapter we suggest prompts to generate writing. All prompts are invitations that can be adapted. Alongside writing practices are fieldwork exercises—on the street, in the library, and with an audio or video recorder. Each chapter also includes ideas for using journals, discussion of craft issues, recommendations for revision, and further development of writing exercises.

Within chapters we consider race, class, gender, and sexual orientation and how each affects how we see and experience another culture. These dimensions crosscut other categories, as does language. Race relations shape history, history affects gender and power, gender permeates language, and language reflects every other part of culture. We hope that readers or group leaders will explore these domains to meet their needs.

We also discuss emotional reactions. Loneliness and fear are a natural part of discovery; both can foster new vision but also leave us unmoored. Fear may function as an alarm or set a dangerous trap. How do we know when that pounding heart is signaling actual danger—and when it is only triggering stereotypes about "the other"? We explore fear in chapter 2, but a variety of emotional responses emerge at every step.

Part Two: Return and Revision

In his Mexico travelogue, *The Lawless Roads*, Graham Greene wrote: "The border means more than a customs house, a passport officer, a man with a gun. Over there, everything is going to be different; life is never going to be quite the same again after your passport has been stamped and you find yourself speechless among the money changers."[8]

The border, of course, works both ways, going and coming back. "Return and Revision" details the links between revision of the work and the life after an experience abroad. This book builds on Greene's belief that after the journey *life is never going to be quite the same again*. How do we find form to communicate the transformation of living abroad? How can we shape the mass of information crammed into our notebooks and on laptops, recorders, and cameras?

Though we discuss revision ideas and craft in each chapter, we focus more extensively on this process in chapter 9. In chapter 10, we turn to literary form. Decisions about genre depend on time, place, audience, and other factors. A blog (edited, of course) sends first impressions to friends and family, while a reflective essay written when we return takes the long view. Portraits of people that begin as thin sketches gain depth and context through revision and the perspective time affords. Small, observed details or bits of conversation that seemed insignificant at first gradually evolve. A year after the experience, you realize that the snapping sound that frightened you one night in Nepal was just a flag flapping in the wind. You finally comprehend that the Spanish fruit seller's formal manner was not rude. In writing, you realize that she needed a few months to warm up, just as you required return market visits to appreciate her. Revision brings to the surface latent understanding.

Travelers no longer disconnect from their own cultures as completely as they once did. In *The Last Train to Zona Verde*, Paul Theroux argues that ease of access and connection has diluted travel. His solution: abandon e-mail, phone, and Facebook while on the road. But Peter Whitfield argues that access can serve good travel writing. "Travel writing must respond," he says, "by becoming sharper, more perceptive, more analytical, more imaginative, cutting through the stereotypes, and understanding the reality behind the images and superficial reports."[9] Regardless of whether we stay connected, encountering "otherness" changes us. Reentry unsettles. After living among rural villagers with one set of clothing, your crowded closet at home demands that you reconsider "necessity." After a season almost anywhere, you might wonder at the abundance in U.S. supermarkets.

Throughout the book, we include examples of how other writers explore self and other, balance the interior and external journey, make decisions about literary form, and achieve cultural depth. We draw from a range of nonfiction that includes memoir, essay, and travelogue as well as ethnography, documentary writing, and literary journalism. As noted earlier, journalists have begun to use ethnographic methods; in turn, social scientists increasingly turn to memoir, essay, and journalistic reportage to tell stories for audiences beyond academia.

Whatever your reasons for traveling or methods you adopt, we urge you to read and research; to watch, listen, and record; to learn different languages; and to explore the landscapes and histories of a people. Above all, we hope that these exercises send you to your notebook or laptop to write. Each literary form offers a vehicle for bringing a cultural encounter to life.

As writers, each of us is, in the words of poet Rainer Maria Rilke, "a perpetual beginner." Yet beginnings do lead somewhere. What follows are signposts to help you navigate and guide others on that journey with you.

I

—

ENCOUNTERING CULTURES

I

—

GETTING READY

The writer abroad needs concrete as well as intangible skills, both of which this book will help you develop. Two capacities are essential: the readiness to embrace a new culture and the discipline to write about it. You may be tempted to just pack and go but advance preparation will foster abilities to help you thrive anywhere from Reykjavik to Vanuatu. Start now, close to home, to explore your own culture, commit to a daily writing practice, and begin advance research.

THE PRACTICE OF WRITING

Notice that we stress discipline over brilliance as essential to a writer. "Talent," said Gustave Flaubert, "is only lengthy patience."[1] Writer and editor Gordon Lish, when asked how he chose students for his fiction writing workshops, said, "I see the notion of talent as quite irrelevant. I see instead perseverance, application, industry, assiduity, will, will, will, desire, desire, desire."[2] Remember this when the inner critic, that shadowy figure we describe in the craft discussion at the end of this chapter, argues that you have nothing to say. Ignore the voice that directs you to the beach instead of the desk. Pledge to write even when you're tired, frustrated, or depressed. Writing daily is akin to weight lifting and regular hikes to prepare for a backpacking trip. Initially, you may not eagerly anticipate that encounter with the blank page but little by little, joy might creep in.

Some practical considerations: notebooks and journals—and increasingly, laptops and iPads—are critical tools for travelers. Consider several types of journals, including a pocket-sized notebook for on-the-street reporting and a larger one for writing at home or on a train or in cafés. Choose lined or unlined, expensive bound books or cheap school copybooks; writing tools are an individual preference. You might prefer a small computer or tablet to register your thoughts in a safe place. Don't expect your memory to guard details you think you'll never forget. Always include dates, times, and places.

Reasons to write while abroad may seem obvious. Of course you want to remember the mastery of Chinese or those rainforest leeches that clung to your legs. But beyond the need for recall, what compels our writing? Francine du Plessix Gray said, "We write out of revenge against reality, to dream and enter the lives of others."[3] In the essay "Why I Write," Terry Tempest Williams includes some widely shared reasons—to record of her thoughts and share them with friends. But she also writes to migrating birds and her own ghosts, as a bow to wilderness and a dance with paradox. When you trust the writing process, unexpected gifts emerge. Tempest Williams ends with: "I write as though I am whispering in the ear of the one I love."[4] Start here with exploring why you write as well as travel.

✔

Writing Exercise One

Dive into your first freewrite with "I write to . . ." or "I write because . . ." Follow that with "I travel to . . ." or "I travel because . . ."

THE JOURNEY'S NARRATOR

This book focuses on nonfiction, which includes essay, memoir, documentary, travel writing, and other genres we explore in chapter 10. But the person who tells the story is not the living, breathing author. The "I" is a narrator shaped on the page, a partial persona. The voice you develop will also reflect a person changed by travel. By the end of this book, the writer who returns will be different from the one who embarked.

Recognizing who you are before you depart is essential. Writing your personal and social history is one way to make that knowledge visible. Writer and filmmaker Julie Checkoway suggests a model in the memoir *Little Sister: Searching for the Shadow World of Chinese Women*. She weaves personal history with the stories of resilience and strength of the women she met while teaching in Shijiazhuang, an industrial town south of Beijing. One woman struggled with a hand disfigured in an accident while working in a truck factory during the Cultural Revolution. Another searched frantically for a foreigner to marry in order to escape China. Alongside the women's stories is Checkoway's chronicle of self-discovery, a pattern common to sojourners abroad. We leave home to seek "the other" but find new parts of ourselves.

Little Sister opens with a description of the small New England town where Checkoway was born the year John Kennedy was assassinated. She lost her mother five years later; her father's silence and inability to face that loss shrouded her world. To keep her occupied, her grandmother sent her out back with a teaspoon to dig to China. This same grandmother would be banished from the house by Checkoway's father, leaving the author bereft. We learn all of this in a few scant pages at the book's start. The setup helps us understand Checkoway's meaning when she writes: "Girls whose mothers disappear can spend their whole lives digging and digging, searching the broad earth for images in near and distant mirrors."[5] We're also prepared for the day when Checkoway, after completing her degree at the Iowa's Writer's Workshop, accepts the challenge from anthropologist Margery Wolf to search for the hidden world of Chinese women.

Checkoway explains further how her heritage and loss of her mother propelled her to seek other cultures. Youth, she says, creates an imprint—a "map" we follow throughout our lives. Depending on the contours of that map, some of us stay in our childhood places; others move outward. But our search is shaped by those internal longings.

As you prepare to leave the familiar living rooms, what is the map you carry? These may reflect the physical world—a deep, mysterious woods where you played as a child compels you to comb forests everywhere. A psychological map charts your place in a large family, or the quest for success embodied in an immigrant story. Cultural maps reflect class and social status. Who gets to travel? Are you the first in your family to go abroad? Where did your ancestors come from—were they fleeing violence or poverty or searching for new work or other opportunities?

✔

Writing Exercise Two

List all the ancestors you remember and where they came from. Write about one, starting with "I am the daughter/son or granddaughter/grandson of . . ."

Then freewrite on the map you use to navigate. Begin with, "I carry with me the map of . . ." Bear in mind that when we "borrow" a writer's structure, we must later remove the scaffolding and find our own form. For example, if you begin with "I carry with me the map," later cut that phrase from your piece. Alternately, you could footnote Julie Checkoway as your inspiration.

CULTURE AS A MAP

Cultural roots. Cultural competency. Multiculturalism. The word "culture" is so ubiquitous that it's hard to remember when it wasn't everyday currency. But the term is also complex, its meanings sometimes contradictory. Critic Raymond Williams wrote, "Culture is one of the two or three most complicated words in the English language."[6] Some still think about capital C Culture: ballet, opera, and the elite arts. But most of us understand culture the way anthropologists have for more than a century as something we absorb growing up. One of the oldest but still helpful definitions comes from Edward B. Tylor's 1871 book, *Primitive Culture*: "Culture or civilization, taken in its wide ethnographic sense, is that complex whole which includes knowledge, belief, art, morals, law, custom, and any other capabilities and habits acquired by man as a member of society."[7]

Williams also noted that "culture is ordinary: that is the first fact. Every human society has its own shape, its own purposes, its own meanings."[8] In this everyday sense, culture defines the rules we internalize unconsciously as we grow up. It's a kind of map, even if it varies among individuals in a culture. People have long been fascinated by folktales of children raised by wolves or actual stories of those living outside a cultural framework. Such tales repel and fascinate. In *Genie: A Scientific Tragedy*, Russ Rymer recounts how the discovery of Genie, left in a dark room in her father's house between infancy and age thirteen, galvanized scientists to ask a question central to understanding humanity: Who would we be without culture? "Unworkable monstrosities," says anthropologist Clifford Geertz, "with very few useful instincts, few recognizable sentiments, and no intellect." Geertz offers his own definition of culture: "Believing, with Max Weber, that man is an animal suspended in webs of significance he himself has spun, I take culture to be those webs."[9]

These "webs of significance" may be regional, racial, class- or gender-based, ethnic, occupational, or religious. They encompass cultures we're suspended in now or were in the past. You may no longer attend religious services yet still consider yourself Jewish or Christian or Muslim. But cultures also shift over time and with our positions in the world. When your family moves from Mumbai to Tennessee, how does your sense as Hindu change? Cultural identity or class status in your home country affects how you view others. How does life for a Catholic in New York City differ from that of a rural villager in El Salvador? Say you're living with a family in Uruguay. Their surroundings—a comfortable house, a new Honda—may mark them as elite, even if they seem middle class. Exploring our own "webs" in advance helps us interpret difference more accurately.

Writing Exercise Three

To get to the heart of a topic, suggests Peter Elbow, write your "first thoughts." Begin a freewrite with "first thoughts on culture." What associations does the word trigger? Follow with a list of the cultures that have shaped you. Tell a story about one influence, beginning with "I remember . . ."—for example, ". . . my grandfather's ranch" or ". . . learning to speak English."

We travel in part to discover something about ourselves, but that self-portrait doesn't always appeal. During a trip to Tokyo in 2002, journalist Alison Buckholtz visited the home of the master bamboo craftsman, Hirokawa-san. She wanted to buy one of his intricately woven bamboo baskets. As an American, Buckholtz thought it "axiomatic that, as travelers, we can partake in the cultural riches around us by purchasing them." She saw Hirokawa-san's studio as a "sort of scaled-back Pier One."[10] To her frustration, Hirokawa-san did not sell his work. Buckholtz's story turns to joy when Hirokawa-san presents the basket as a parting gift. This is the heart of travel, she says, this sort of surprise. But Buckholtz likely didn't anticipate that her new learning would include this reflection of Americans as relentless consumers. We can't know in advance what mix of joy and chagrin will come with travel. But if we understand our home cultures, we'll be better prepared for sometimes vexing discoveries.

THE SHAPING FORCE OF PLACE

You could begin, as Checkoway does, with writing about an important place in your past. The physical isolation of coastal "Puritan towns" defined her experience. Equally important was the social landscape where "spunky cheerleaders gave birth out of wedlock" before they transformed to grouchy clerks in orthopedic shoes working in needlework stores.[11] The world Checkoway describes helps us feel her urgency to flee.

Familiar places and their smells, sights, and sounds mark us in unconscious as well as conscious ways. The smell of manure could trigger nostalgia for someone who grew up on a farm, but it might disgust an urbanite. A corner restaurant with barred windows could frighten strangers but connect others with the comfort of neighbors trading gossip over coffee. Memories are often fragments, not full-fledged stories. Writer David Duncan calls these "river teeth," an analogy based on the natural world. When felled trees disintegrate into a river, knotty bits of wood refuse to break down. Duncan likens these dense "cross-grained whorls" to stubborn memories that stay with us "long after the straight-grained narrative material that housed them has washed away."[12]

Some of our "river teeth" carry mixed associations. Here, Pico Iyer evokes his early years in England: "It is the light, on summer evenings, drifting on till 9 P.M. or later. . . . It is the scratchy smell of grass, the thunk of bat on cricket ball. . . . It is, of course, nostalgia— geography's déjà vu—that makes up a large part of what we call the 'sacred.'"[13]

Iyer describes a contradictory aspect of home: it may be the place we feel compelled to flee but also long to revisit. Nostalgia for sacred places seeps into a person. Iyer has traveled the world and now lives in Japan. Yet the England of his boyhood still calls to him.

We'll explore landscape in chapter 6, but these initial exercises will help you examine a sense of place before encountering new environments.

Writing Exercise Four

List places that (1) you have considered "home," (2) are sacred, (3) you longed to flee, and (4) you yearn to return to. Pick one and describe it in detail, starting with "I remember . . ." or as Iyer does, "It is . . ."

THE WRITER AS WITNESS

Once you arrive in Cambodia or Argentina or Finland, you'll notice everything. The allure of the unfamiliar enlivens our senses and our minds. But how can we learn to do the same in our own neighborhoods, places we see so regularly that we don't in fact see them anymore? A Russian term *ostranenie* refers to artistic techniques meant to startle viewers or readers into seeing the familiar in new ways. "Defamiliarization"—a term coined in the early twentieth century by Victor Shklovsky in reference to poetry—can reframe our daily experiences. Documentary photographer Dorothea Lange described a camera as a tool that teaches us to see without a camera. Similarly, writing is a tool for learning to observe daily life even without a pen in hand. Jotting down notes records experience but the practice is a feedback loop: the more you record, the more you notice. Your noticing makes the familiar into something novel.

Central to documenting social life is the notion of witness. The word has multiple meanings, some particular to distinct religious traditions. To witness can mean to testify, account for, be present at an event, or affirm religious beliefs. We see, record, and attend to our environment with heightened awareness when we think of ourselves as witnesses. An observer can compile facts; a witness is engaged, reaching for deeper truths. Add "bearing" to "witness" and new meanings arise. "Bearing" implies weight: to give birth to, support, yield, tolerate, endure. At home and abroad, witnessing prompts awareness of society's margins and of lives we can't see or feel until we move beyond observation.

Perhaps you've never thought about that old man living out of a shopping cart a few blocks from your home. Maybe you've stopped considering the day laborers lined up downtown and whether they may or may not eat today. We grow inured to hardship in order to survive the "compassion fatigue" common to contemporary life. But what insight, understanding, and empathy do we sacrifice when we stop seeing what surrounds us? We may also miss joy— the pleasure on the face of the woman reading in the park, of the kids leaping for a basketball.

Lives of privilege may be as invisible as those marked by hardship, though for different reasons. Ted Conover's *Whiteout: Lost in Aspen*, which explores the world of the town's wealthy residents, offers a different sort of witness. To gather material, he took jobs—taxi driver, local newspaper reporter—that put him in close touch with his subjects and their lives—an approach we'll explore in more detail in the next section.

BECOMING A PARTICIPANT OBSERVER

We want to feel connected as witnesses to another culture and its people. But to see from another point of view, we also need to suspend judgment. This is the heart of ethnographic fieldwork, a practice that combines engaged observation with participation in cultural life. Imagine yourself invited to a religious ritual in a new place. How do you figure out when to stand or sit? Should you join in the prayers if you're a nonbeliever? Anthropologists, folklorists, sociologists, and documentarians often spend between several months and many years in new settings, whether close to home or abroad. As participant observers, they have a dual agenda of involvement and detachment. They create a place in the group, learn the language, participate in social life, take field notes, and finally, analyze and write. "Ethnography" stems from the Greek "ethnos," people or nation, and "graphy," writing; the term refers to both the process and its product.

Because we're rooted in our own cultural worldviews, seeing from an insider's point of view is an ideal. "Thinking like a native" eludes us, especially since natives of anywhere are a diverse group with widely varied views. Culture is not homogeneous. But we can strive to see as others do through fieldwork, interviews, and in-depth research on the ground and in the library. Partial understanding is still a form of knowledge.

Margaret Mead describes the task of the fieldworker—or any culturally alive traveler or student—as follows: "One must live all day in a maze of relationships without being caught in the maze. And above all, one must wait for events to reveal much that must be learned . . . the fieldworker records, learns—and waits. But it is always an active waiting, a readiness in which all his senses are alert to whatever may happen, expected or unexpected, in the next five minutes—or in an hour, a week, a month from now."[14]

This dedication leads to greater depth. Some ethnographers find such awareness in their own country or community. In *Evicted: Poverty and Profit in the American City*, sociologist Matthew Desmond uncovers devastating inequality in the U.S. housing world. While his statistics shock, it's the stories of evicted families, especially single mothers with children, that slam us up against the reality of poverty. Desmond lived in a trailer among people being evicted; he also came to know landlords. His depiction of both groups in complex, evocative detail fulfills his definition of ethnography as "what you do when you try to understand people by allowing their lives to mold your own as fully and genuinely as possible."[15]

Desmond uses descriptive details and other tools of the creative nonfiction writer to create his portraits of poverty. When Arlene, a Milwaukee, Wisconsin, woman whose life he follows, is evicted, she opts for "curb" eviction where everything is piled onto the sidewalk. "Her mattresses. A floor-model television. Her copy of *Don't Be Afraid to Discipline*. Her nice glass dining table and the lace tablecloth that fit just-so." Desmond's list juxtaposes this vestige of comfortable living—a lace tablecloth—with a mother's struggle to keep children in line. The author rarely inserts his own voice, though one journal entry reveals his struggle: "I feel dirty, collecting these stories and hardships like so many trophies."[16] We discover only at the end of the book that Desmond's own parents were evicted. His work realizes the best tradition of ethnography—witness focused outward, written with clarity, vivid description, and apt characterization.

While ethnographers like Desmond write like journalists, some journalists now turn to ethnographic methods. Writer Lauren Kessler describes the traditional approach: "You make a few calls. You frame the story in your mind, then you go looking to fill the frame. You zip into people's lives, disrupt their routines, ask a lot of questions and leave."[17] In contrast, Kessler says, she looks to ethnographers, who don't come with "the story" already in place. Rather, they stay open to whatever the story might be. They listen and watch, slowly entering a community. Kessler follows this method in her books, including her sensitive account of working in an Alzheimer's center, *Finding Life in the Land of Alzheimer's: One Daughter's Hopeful Story*.

Ted Conover specializes in immersion journalism. We cited his work in Aspen above; he's also worked as a corrections officer in Sing Sing and traveled with hoboes, Mexican migrants crossing into the United States with so-called coyotes, loggers in Peru, and truckers in Kenya. He calls immersion journalism a "cousin" to ethnography, citing his undergraduate anthropology courses as inspiration. Though Conover writes in the first person, his work, like Desmond's and Kessler's, focuses outward. First person can also reveal the writer's unavoidable bias, what Robin Hemley describes as "all that baggage that makes up the writer's personality: his or her memories, culture, and opinions."[18] Journalists are bound by different ethical and professional rules than ethnographers, but both need to account for their baggage, just as you are doing in preparation for your journey.

The challenges of participant observation in your own culture differ from those you'll encounter overseas. But both ask us to see in new ways. Immerse yourself in any local situation and use the concept of *ostranenie* to rediscover the familiar.

Fieldwork Exercise One

Pick an accessible everyday site near your home, such as a park, a bus stop, or a coffee shop. Observe for half an hour. Write about what you notice, starting with "I would like to describe . . ." What did you fail to see before? Do people speak to their neighbors? Offer seats to the elderly? Try to uncover the unstated rules for behavior. Return to the site on a regular basis—at least three to five times.

SEEING OURSELVES THROUGH
THE EYES OF OTHERS

One way to uncover your own culture's rules is through the vision of visitors, recent immigrants, and residents of other countries. As Alison Buckholtz discovered, the portrait isn't always rosy. In "A View from Canada," writer Margaret Atwood describes her country's noisy southern neighbor as she saw them during a trip to India. While in New Delhi, she visited separate enclaves of Canadians and Americans. Canadians filled their house with local decorations and served her Indian food. In contrast, the Americans created a separate miniature United States. She describes their walled compound: "We were let in to do some shopping . . . and once the gate had closed, you were in Syracuse, New York. Hot dogs, hamburgers, cokes and rock music surrounded you. Americans enter the outside world the way they landed on the moon, with their own

oxygen tanks of American air strapped to their backs and their pro-
tective spacesuits firmly in place."[19]

In *A Small Place*, Jamaica Kincaid writes in the second person
to address the quintessential tourist visiting her home country
of Antigua. As a European or North American—"to be frank,
white"—you will move through customs quickly. Your bags will
not be searched like those of Antiguan blacks coming home with
"cardboard boxes of much needed cheap clothes." You will survey
the green landscape and pray it won't rain, as you escape harsh, cold
North American or European winters. That desperate Antiguans,
who suffer constant drought, might seek rain, "must never cross
your mind."[20] Though Kincaid's characterization might make a
visitor squirm, it tilts assumptions in powerful ways.

It's important to know how residents of a new place see you—not
just your individual history but how you reflect your nation, religion,
gender, and class position. You can start before you leave home.

Fieldwork Exercise Two

Contact an immigrant—a recently arrived or long-term resident—
perhaps by doing volunteer work through a local program. Visit several
times to establish trust before setting up an interview: How does he or
she view your culture? How does this new setting and its people compare to his or her homeland? See chapter 5 on portraits for a discussion
of ethical issues, and chapter 4 on documentary forms for effective interview strategies.

LOOKING AHEAD: WHAT WE CARRY

"Few of us travel without some kind of baggage be it in the head or
the hand," writes global educator Michael Woolf. He describes the
idea of Europe in the American mind, one based on pop culture and

the vision of writers from Mark Twain to Henry Miller. Europe, for many American students venturing abroad, writes Woolf, is "Disney's Magic Kingdom and it is High Art and it is cheap red wine."[21]

Stereotypes can fill our baggage, hard as we try to shed them. Before leaving, consider your ideas about food, weather, people, and language. Where do they come from? If you grew up in 1950s America, your trip to Cuba might be shaped by the ghost of Desi Arnaz as Ricky Ricardo on *I Love Lucy*.

What we literally carry also reveals expectations. As you prepare to leave, consult your list of "essentials." Do you really need your tiny French-press coffeemaker? In *The Things They Carried*, Tim O'Brien excavates the baggage of U.S. soldiers in Vietnam. Some deemed cigarettes necessary, others Kool-Aid packets and chewing gum. Mundane, you might think. But O'Brien accretes details to prepare us for what's coming—the broader, emotionally charged subject triggered by the narrow subject. He writes: "They carried all the emotional baggage of men who might die. Grief, terror, love, longing—these were intangibles, but the intangibles had their own mass and specific gravity, they had tangible weight. . . . They carried the common secret of cowardice barely restrained, the instinct to run or freeze or hide, and in many respects this was the heaviest burden of all."[22]

Writing can uncover conscious as well as unconscious expectations in the baggage that we all carry.

Writing Exercise Five

Make a list of material goods you consider essential for this trip. Chose two or three items from your list. Freewrite about what would happen if you left them behind. Then make a visual map of the place to which you're traveling, clustering ideas around a circle with "Thailand" or "Kyrgyzstan" at its center. Include images and stories from film, television, literature, and news you've seen or read. What does the map reveal about your expectations?

Fieldwork Exercise Three

Return to the interview you did with a recent refugee or immigrant. Add questions about what he or she carried with them from their country and why. What do the things they carried say about their values and needs?

LOOKING AHEAD: RESEARCH

You've turned an interpretive lens on your own culture to uncover assumptions. Now consider what you don't yet know about where you're headed. Fidel Castro is a familiar name, but how many Americans recognize Cuban revolutionary philosopher and poet José Martí? Learning about an unknown destination can feel overwhelming, but advance exploration will enhance your overseas experience immeasurably.

Begin with library and Internet resources at home. Read newspapers, many of which are online. If you don't yet know the language, start with an article a week, keeping vocabulary lists. Add one of the many global news sources available online in English. Travel literature and guidebooks are practical tools and cultural reflections of how visitors view or have viewed a place. Ask for advice from local specialists and librarians if a web search doesn't turn up enough material. You can't read everything, so select varied viewpoints.

Travel writing that offers such diversity dates back to the Greeks. Herodotus, one of the first known historians, has also been called an early ethnographer for his systematic collection of materials, especially oral accounts. His belief that cultural norms, *nomos* in Greek, varied over time and across cultures, was revolutionary for the period. Such broad-minded thinking waxed and waned over the centuries. Many Westerners writing about "others," argues Peter Whitfield, conveyed a "triumphalist world-view" tied to colonialism.[23] Yet this was not a singular stance. For example, the British writer Mary Kingsley revealed complex views in her best-selling chronicle, *Travels in West Africa* (1897). While she supported British indirect rule, she also criticized Christian missions and defended practices such as polygamy. Or consider the intrepid Isabelle Eberhardt, who left Switzerland for Algeria in 1897, converted to Islam, and dressed as a man. She left behind anticolonialist writings that defied the attitudes of her European contemporaries.

You might consult Ibn Battuta's work on Africa and the Middle East. One of history's greatest travelers, Battuta recorded extensive journeys through the Islamic world and beyond. Before Battuta died in 1377 at age seventy-three in Tangier, he had covered seventy-five thousand miles across Africa, the Middle East, parts of Europe, and Asia. He wrote it all down in anecdotal and emotional accounts. Follow Battuta with Edith Wharton's *In Morocco* (1920). Reflecting her background, Wharton condemns what she saw as primitive attitudes and conditions, especially regarding women in harems. Yet she described Morocco as enchanting, explored its concepts of time, and celebrated its architecture.

In the last hundred years, many travel writers have shifted their stance as they try to understand and evoke cultural complexity. Still, earlier chronicles left lingering traces. We need to investigate portrayals from the past to understand the present. But we must be wary of "presentism"—judging the writers of previous eras by today's standards. To get a full picture, look for insider and outsider versions, travel stories from diverse time periods, and those by writers of different genders.

☑

Writing Exercise Six

Choose three works by travel writers whose work spans the course of a century. To explore China, you might include *Thunder out of China*, a 1946 eyewitness account by two *Time-Life* correspondents, Theodore H. White and Annalee Jacoby. The book, one of the first reports on China's transition to Communism, examines the tumultuous decades before and after World War II in the context of Chinese history. Peter Hessler's *Or-*

acle Bones: A Journey through Time in China (2007) tells a broader story of
China's transformation over the past hundred years. Finally, you could
include Lijia Zhang's 2011 coming-of-age memoir, *"Socialism Is Great!"
A Worker's Memoir of the New China.* Zhang grew up in China, helped
organize the Tiananmen Square demonstrations of 1989, and is now a
journalist. Take notes on questions, surprises, and ongoing concerns and
copy quotes you can later use as writing prompts. Then research (1) the
authors' bios and (2) the national boundaries and political scene in the era
of each book's setting. Record your first thoughts on how each writer
reflects the country. Be sure to note other books and resources that will
aid your detective work.

Think critically. Before Joanne led a study program to Australia,
she read a literary magazine whose editors claimed they could
find no Aboriginal writers for a special issue related to the Sydney
Olympics. Yet she soon discovered a thriving Aboriginal writing
scene in Australia. Novels such as *Follow the Rabbit-Proof Fence*,
which would soon become an acclaimed film, had been published
years before. Commerce, politics, and history shape what we think
of as central or "available."

Film has gained global importance, politically and artistically.
Nigeria's Nollywood now ranks just behind Hollywood and Bol-
lywood as the world's third-largest producer of feature films. Look
into the history of film wherever you're going, searching YouTube,
online sites, and local and university libraries.

Read ahead from a range of literature. Is your destination dominated by oral tradition? Fiction, nonfiction, or poetry? Check
out collections on different cultures such as Trinity University
Press's "writers on writing" series, The Writer's World. Trans-
lations introduce us to new writers and ideas. Some anthologies
such as *Viajes en México* (*Mexican Journeys*) juxtapose "crónicas
mexicanas"—Mexican accounts—with "crónicas extranjeras"—
those by foreigners.[24] Think beyond the writing itself to ask who

controls publishing and whether writers have access to translators. Iceland, for example, offers grants for translation and distribution of writers' work. Explore different national priorities vis-à-vis the arts. Ireland famously exempts from tax a certain amount of an artist's income from work deemed to have cultural merit.

Cultures conceive of visual art in vastly different ways. In chapter 3, we delve into visual language, but you can prepare by finding important arts and architectural sites in places you'll visit. Include museums, galleries, monuments, significant buildings, and established locations. Be sure to branch out to street art, folk culture, and nontraditional locations and forms. Investigate the biographies of noteworthy artists in the region.

CRAFT DISCUSSION: DISCIPLINE AND THE INNER CRITIC

Why does it seem so hard to develop a daily writing practice? Writers routinely confess they'll do anything to avoid writing—laundry, yard work, and especially, web surfing. There's more at work here than sheer laziness.

Consider one of the strongest deterrents to our desired discipline: that pesky inner critic who insists we have nothing original to say. "Do you know how many students were bored in Hebrew class?" whispers that voice as you describe your early experiences with new languages. All writers battle a sense of futility at times. Yet another voice counters. "In every work of genius," said Emerson, "we recognize our own rejected thoughts."[25] In her essay "The Watcher at the Gate," writer Gail Godwin tells a story of confronting her inner critic. She was writing a novel in which her heroine was dreaming, when suddenly, "I lost faith in my own invention and rushed to an 'authority' to check whether she could have such a dream." Godwin finally found a letter from Freud to Schiller that contained a liberating idea: "In the case of a creative mind, it seems to me, the intellect has withdrawn its watchers from the gates, and the ideas rush in pell-mell, and only then does it review and inspect the multitude."[26] When you come to revision and editing, the inner critic will aid the process. For now, banish that voice and free yourself to explore the full range of possibilities.

Writing Exercise Seven

Describe your inner critic. Give him or her an attitude and visual shape. Write the critic a letter asking why he or she won't let you create. Follow with a list of subjects the critic considers taboo.

REVISION

You've explored your own cultural background and recorded first thoughts on where you're headed. Let that writing sit until close to your departure and then revisit those freewrites. Revision, literally to "see again," can extend through many drafts. First review your writing, expand with additional freewrites, and then cut what feels extraneous. Your writing will grow and shrink, accordion-like. Revision and editing happen at both the macro and micro levels, which we explore in detail in chapter 9. For now, simply revisit an earlier freewrite.

Revision Exercise One

(1) Return to your "first thoughts on culture" (writing exercise 3, above, this chapter). After the passage of time and your experiments with participant observation, what do you think now? You might begin with: "Further thoughts on culture." (2) Return to the freewrite about your ancestors. If you wrote "I am the daughter of . . . ," now add a generational layer: "I am the granddaughter of . . ." or "the grandfather of . . ."

If you're writing for a particular audience, you may have a structure in mind. Otherwise, you don't need to decide on literary form yet. But if you want to experiment, essays—from the French verb *essayer*—"to try"—are a great place to start. You don't need to be an expert. New thoughts may emerge *as* you write, but a trusty essay form lets you improvise within a structure. Essays, like most creative nonfiction, combine storytelling and reflection, telling what happened and musing on the meaning of events.

Experiment with Form—Try a Personal Essay

First, return to the freewrite about ancestral heritage that you just revised for revision exercise 1 (or chose another one in which you told a story). Rewrite that story in the present tense as though it were happening now. You might begin with "I'm standing in my grandmother's kitchen . . ." Write for a page or two, reread what you've written, then begin a freewrite with "Looking back now . . ." You have the beginnings of an essay that combines story and reflection.

The chapters that follow will help you to negotiate new languages and landscapes, create individual portraits, probe religious and political beliefs, and use social media and documentary forms in ethical ways. We hope that these and other abilities become embedded through a lifetime of travel. Concrete skills meld to less tangible but equally essential ones: an open heart and a willingness to suffer humiliation as we learn. As we revise our writing, we also "re-see" our attitudes and understanding. If we record our blunders, we'll glimpse the path to understanding.

The commitment to writing is central to preparation and to travel. The dancer and choreographer Twyla Tharp argues that daily discipline extends across genres of expression: "This is no different for any creative individual whether it's a painter finding his way to the easel or a medical researcher returning to the laboratory. The routine is as much a part of the creative process as the lightning bolt of inspiration (perhaps more). And it is available to everyone. If creativity is a habit, then the best creativity is a result of good work habits. They are the nuts and bolts of dreaming."[27]

DISCOVERING NEW CULTURES

Sometimes we travel with a purpose, other times for unconscious or mysterious reasons. In every case, travel yields discovery. Ernestine McHugh's memoir *Love and Honor in the Himalayas* recounts her time conducting fieldwork among the Gurung people of Nepal in the 1970s and 1980s. McHugh was a student of Gregory Bateson, renowned anthropologist and the third husband of Margaret Mead. McHugh set out to study death rituals, having lost her mother at fourteen. She would confront more death while abroad, triggering revelations about herself as well as this new culture. Writing her memoir years later, she found deeper connections between personal loss and learning about death in Nepal. Bateson's teachings had primed her to seek such correspondence. "One day," she writes, "he gave us each a Rilke poem and sent us into the forest to find a leaf with the same structure."[1] Throughout her life abroad and in writing about it, McHugh searched for relationships between divergent worlds. A poem and a leaf. Affinities across cultures can teach us what is wholly different yet somehow alike in human experience.

DEPARTURES AND FIRST IMPRESSIONS

McHugh embarked for Nepal besieged by uncertainty. "I buckled my seatbelt and looked out at the dark runway, marked by blue lamps. I wondered what I was doing, going so far away alone."[2] We, too, sometimes wonder at our motives at the start of a journey. Perhaps you remember the first time you flew to Buenos Aires, rode a high-speed train in Japan, or watched the shore recede from a ship set for Europe. Fear and exhilaration may merge as we depart. Of her first flight, McHugh writes, "There was a stewardess standing in a blue suit in the middle of the narrow aisle. She had black hair and a small round hat. I heard the thump as they closed the door, the click of the lock that secured it. I looked out into the dark again and began to cry."[3] The attendant's blue suit and hat, the sound of the door locking: these build a foundation for McHugh's emotional journey. She follows with descriptions of an abominable snowman on the side of the Royal Nepal Airlines plane, and an "air hostess" passing out candles. These details move us quickly from the now routine ritual of takeoff to a less familiar time and place. We don't yet know how immersion in Nepalese life will affect McHugh. But we have shared her departure; her tears and uncertainty stay with us.

In chapter 1, we surveyed our own cultural backgrounds, finding ways to make the familiar strange. What similar tools aid our encounter with a foreign world? You may be tempted to iron out or bypass what feels unsettling. But difference is our greatest teacher, argues Mexican writer Carlos Fuentes. Growing up in the United States, Mexico, and Chile when his father was a diplomat, Fuentes learned that "cultures are not isolated, and perish when deprived of contact with what is different and challenging. . . . No culture . . . retains its identity in isolation; identity is attained in contact, in contrast, in breakthrough."[4]

As you shape the story of your own breakthrough, a compelling entry point is essential. You might start as McHugh did with your launch via plane, boat, car, or bicycle. Or your initial journal entry might describe impressions that form pell-mell. Perhaps your first morning in Lima, Peru, filled with traffic noise, children shouting, and a vendor hawking orange juice outside your window as you woke up. Maybe a dust storm at the N'Djamena airport turned day to night. You may think you'll remember these details forever, but we often don't register what we've seen or think until we begin to write. The poet William Stafford noted, "A writer is not so much someone who has something to say as he is someone who has found a process that will bring about new things he would not have thought of if he had not started to say them."[5]

Sometimes an everyday experience suddenly seems novel, demanding new vocabulary. In *The Palace of the Snow Queen*, Barbara Sjoholm describes cold and snow unlike any she'd experienced:

I arrived in Swedish Lapland at two fifteen in the afternoon on the overnight train from Stockholm. Mid-November and already it was dusk, the *blue hour*, when the slate-colored snow looks colder than white. The five others who stepped off in Kiruna, from the almost-empty train grinding on to the Norwegian border, vanished into cars or the one taxi. The station was deserted; not a single traveler remained to ask for directions to my hotel. A fluster of snow filled the air—strange, hectic snow, blowing in the refrigerator-cold light of a solitary streetlamp.[6]

Notice how Sjoholm describes the "slate-colored snow" as "colder than white," mixing color with physical sensation. Pairing unlikely elements helps forge new vision. A poem and a leaf.

Writing Exercise One

Write a scene that details your travel to a new place. Begin with the prompt: "Travel with me to . . ." Describe in as much detail as possible what surrounds you. In the spirit of Barbara Sjoholm's description of snow, register your first impressions in ways that invite a fresh perspective.

CULTURAL LOGIC: IDENTITY AND DAILY LIFE

In chapter 1, we cited Raymond Williams's idea that culture is "ordinary." African American writer James Baldwin, in a classic essay from *Notes of a Native Son* echoes this thought: "One had, in short, to come into contact with an alien culture in order to understand that a culture was not a community basket-weaving project, nor yet an act of God; was something neither desirable nor undesirable in itself." His essays suggest ways to think about ourselves in unfamiliar terrain—for him, an awareness filtered through a prism of the racism he fled the United States to escape. Baldwin lived in France for eight years, remaining a part-time resident until his death in 1987. "I had come to Paris originally with a little over forty dollars in my pockets," he wrote, "and no grasp whatever of the French language. It developed, shortly, that I had no grasp of the French character either."[7] Yet over time, he learned to characterize his hosts even as they characterized him. "The French," he wrote, "consider that all Negroes arrive from America trumpet-laden and twinkle-toed, bearing scars so unutterably painful that all of the glories of the French Republic may not suffice to heal them."[8]

In "Equal in Paris," Baldwin raises an essential question about identity in a new culture. The essay recounts his eight days in a Paris jail after he was arrested for possession of a bed sheet stolen by an acquaintance and deposited in his hotel room. The French authorities, he writes, didn't see him as "a despised black man" but only as *Américain*. He thus found himself shaken, wondering not "*what* I was, but *who*," unable to act without the strategies created to survive racism in the United States.[9]

Baldwin relates a story of individual confusion in a specific time and place: an American black man in Paris in the late 1940s. But he also expresses universal dimensions of oppression. The emotional punch comes in the essay's final pages after a lawyer friend aids his release. Baldwin describes the courtroom scene whose celebratory "merriment" he found chilling. "It could only remind me of the laughter I had often heard at home . . . this laughter is the laughter of those who consider themselves to be at a safe remove from all the wretched, for whom the pain of the living is not real. I had heard it so often in my native land that I had resolved to find a place where I would never hear it any more [sic]. In some deep, black, stony and liberating way, my life, in my own eyes, began during that first year in Paris, when it was borne in on me that this laughter is universal and can never be stilled."[10]

You may not have suffered at home as Baldwin did yet you might still arrive abroad and feel disoriented. Who are you in this setting? How do you adapt and write about events you may not understand or even find objectionable? Any aspect of culture might seem bizarre at first. But keep in mind that each has its own logic. "Cultural relativism" is central to cross-cultural exploration. All forms of relativism involve seeing something—morals or meaning, for example—in relation to a distinct framework—a culture, language, or historical period. The concept is sometimes misinterpreted as a fuzzy sort of "anything goes," implying that there are no standards. In fact, trying to grasp a culture on its own terms requires discipline and a grounded understanding. While globalization and international human rights complicate the picture in important ways, cultural relativism persists as an idea and goal. A respect for difference can coexist with universal principles.

PUBLIC AND PRIVATE DOMAINS

We learn from immersion in both domains. But if you live with a family or find other ways into the private realm, you'll master cultural rules more quickly. Ernestine McHugh describes her first encounter with the woman who will be her adopted mother during life with the Gurung people:

"Have you a mother and a father?" she [Lalita] asked.

"No mother. I have a father." I said.

"Your mother died?" she asked, hanging her head to one side and closing her eyes, tongue out in a mime of death.

"Yes," I said . . . Lalita drew on her cigarette and passed it to me.

"You stay here," she said, "I'll be your mother." I blinked. I drew on the cigarette and passed it back. . . .

"Me mother, you daughter," she said in Nepali, pointing.

"Me daughter, you mother," I repeated.

"With deepest thanks," she said formally.

Thus began my long and eventful association with a Gurung community.[11]

Barbara Sjoholm creates a sense of place through novel use of language. James Baldwin poses questions about the shifting nature of identity. McHugh sets an anguished departure scene and then uses dialogue to introduce the human relationships that gave meaning to her life in Nepal. In each case, we experience the writer's initial emotions: confusion, angst, hints of loneliness. But we're also set up for the "breakthrough" to understanding that Carlos Fuentes describes.

Whether you're in Russia for a year or just passing through Australia or Malawi, one domain is central to public and private life: food. Many travelogues take shape around shopping for ingredients, cooking, eating, and haunting markets that brim with sensory detail. Food stalls and restaurants—every part of social life associated with food—beckon us with sounds, smells, and visual details. Markets also mix food with clothing, utensils, tools, and modern electronics, sometimes carried on the backs of animals such as camels or llamas.

Consider how veteran journalist Susan Orlean describes the market fairgrounds in El Jadida, Morocco: "A roar floated over the fairground; it was the combined chatter of hundreds of buyers and sellers haggling, and the smack and thump of boxes being opened and sacks being slapped down to be filled, and vendors hollering

for attention and a blast of Moroccan music playing out of an un-
attended laptop computer that was hooked to man-size speakers,
beneath a tent of fabric cut from a Nokia cell-phone billboard."[12]
Notice how Orlean mixes the market traditions with the impro-
vised modernity of the billboard tent and sets the scene through a
cacophony of sounds.

Writing Exercise Two

Take a walk through the city, town, or countryside of a new place. Use
all of your senses as you write down details, then do a freewrite beginning with "I remember the sound, taste, smell of . . ." Note the way
Susan Orlean uses words like "smack," "thump," and "slapped" to create
sounds on the page.

You've probably faced foods you were loath to eat while traveling.
Dogs and other animals domesticated in the West are considered
edible in some places, a practice abhorrent to those who love their
pets. Visitors to the United States may recoil at hot dogs, peanut
butter, and other Americans favorites. One food blogger described
a ubiquitous American dessert as boiled animal hide, bones, and
garish chemicals—a novel vision of Jell-O. All societies create di-
chotomies, argued anthropologist Claude Lévi-Strauss, that reflect
nature versus culture. The "raw and the cooked" is one central division that forces us to ponder what we consider "natural" or "civ-
ilized."

Perhaps you can't identify the glob of fat on your plate. All
good travelers know the rule: eat what's served. To do otherwise is
rude. But that doesn't mean it's easy. In her essay "Lard Is Good for
You," Alden Jones describes her craving for raw vegetables while
living in Costa Rica. She watched the fresh broccoli from the fields
join big spoonfuls of lard in the frying pan. "I ate the soggy, eggy

broccoli already planning how I would sneak out in the morning with my Swiss army knife, saw off a fresh stalk, and relish it raw as I ate it hidden among the coffee bushes."[13] Jones hears two voices in her head, another view of the traveler-tourist distinction. "Eat the lard and respect local customs," says the Traveler. "Head to the beach for some tasty gringo food," says the Tourist. Jones layers the humorous parts of her stories with commentary on the politics of food. The Costa Rican government initially decreed lard essential in order to add some fat to the national diet of rice and beans. But when a young man in the community dies, reputedly from the heart-clogging lard, everything changes.

On Ernestine McHugh's first morning in Nepal, she awakened to the faces of village children. They brought her tea boiled with ginger, cardamom, and sugar, the bitterness of the tea further cut by buffalo milk. She later learned how rarely anyone had tea with expensive sugar; the family normally used salt. Her first lesson about Nepalese generosity came through food.

Hospitality is a universal notion, but one with variable elements. A U.S. student in Barcelona may have to dine at 11 P.M. while the inverse of a 5:30 dinner in Wisconsin might horrify a Spanish student. Food can generate ethical dilemmas. A host family may bend to vegetarian or other needs but still be perplexed or hurt by the request. Families often stretch budgets to accommodate visitors or long-term guests such as students. Meat, sometimes scarce and expensive, may be saved for visitors. To reject it can create hurt and misunderstanding.

If you're a vegetarian, how sturdy are your beliefs? Do you avoid alcohol at home? Does cultural adaptation trump religious or ethical rules about what to eat? You may find yourself being more pliant or far more observant than you'd imagined.

Alcohol may present dilemmas if you're a Muslim visitor to an Italian family or the inverse. Even if everyone recognizes the religious restrictions, they may perceive them as flexible. Beyond cultural rules, you may have physical limitations with alcohol or certain foods. We discuss ethics in more detail in chapter 7. As sojourners abroad, we want to expand our vision and experience but also avoid harm to others or ourselves.

Writing Exercise Three

Describe a meal where you encountered something you didn't want to or couldn't eat or drink. Use sensory details of smell, taste, and sight to recapture the experience.

THE UNEXPECTED, UNEXPLAINED, AND EMOTIONALLY VOLATILE

Sometimes we struggle to describe something mundane that suddenly seems different, as Barbara Sjoholm found with snow. But more often, the opposite occurs: we confront something beyond our framework for understanding. How do you chronicle such experiences? *In Mama Lola: A Vodou Priestess in Brooklyn*, anthropologist Karen McCarthy Brown describes her immersion in the world of Haitian Vodou. As an ethnographer, she observes and analyzes. But she also enters this world as a participant, eventually marrying Papa Ogou, one of the Vodou spirits. McCarthy Brown is careful not to claim a degree of authority on Vodou that exceeds her experience. But she also captures the knowledge that "exists in the seam between two cultures, where the various strands of the fabric can never be disentangled."[14] Here she recounts her first meeting with Papa Ogou through his possession of Alourdes (Mama Lola): "Alourdes sighed and reached for the rum bottle to refuel her small fire. Again, there was intense concentration, and this time it worked. Barely intense tremors became intense shaking, and then the energy shot out her arms and legs, making them do a stiff staccato dance in the air. When the shaking stopped, Alourdes's body was drawn up straight, and keen black eyes were staring at me with interest. Papa Ogou had arrived."[15]

Ernestine McHugh describes an event that happened after the death of a friend in Nepal. Lying in bed, she felt something drop onto her body. It felt like a small animal walking across her chest, its paw pressing into her flesh. But when it jumped down, there was no sound, nor were the doors or windows open; in fact, there was nothing there. McHugh could find no explanation within her own cultural logic. Her family members told her that such events occur because "death creates a space . . . where uncanny things can enter."[16]

In both examples, the writer's voice is balanced, telling us what she observed and experienced. Neither writer reduces the complexity of another cultural system to Western thinking. Part of the power of both books rests on the equilibrium between possible interpretations and storytelling without judgment. We are witnesses as well as interpreters.

Perhaps Karen McCarthy Brown and Ernestine McHugh were initially uneasy or afraid immersed in events outside their own frames of reference. Fear is logical when confronting the unknown. Additionally, the fear of some travelers is justified when they face physical danger because of their race, sexual orientation, or other reasons. Beyond fear, other emotions will emerge as you travel. You may feel outrage and anger at events you observe or at things that happen to you. Maybe you saw children living on the streets or people huddled in refugee camps. Perhaps you inadvertently provoked someone. What kind of writing re-creates the complexity of emotion?

Consider Patricia Hampl's essay, "Pilgrim," which recounts a startling encounter in an East Jerusalem souk. She was on a friendship tour with a group from Minneapolis. Standing before a spice stall in the souk, Hampl tried to be a sensitive tourist, smiling at the young seller. Then she saw her companion raise her camera. Invisible to the photographer, the boy shook his head no, frowning. It happened quickly, Hampl writes. "The boy said something harsh, and finding no hope of getting the attention of the woman taking the picture, he turned to me. He said something again, hissed across the dazzling table of his wares. Then, he spat. A sharp, targeted bullet of projectile fury. It hit me sharp in the eye, exactly where he intended, I think." Afterward, the author felt calm with "that uncanny knowing of real experience—*Ah, so this is why I came, for this. Real travel wants to be dangerous.*"[17] Travel can teach us about our own hubris, about unequal power, and about emotions triggered by the presence or actions of other travelers.

What starts as fear, outrage, or other emotion triggers strong writing. We are most alert in places that unnerve us. The anxious feeling you get in a crowded train car or when you witness human anguish or surprise may be a "nerve point." If you can identify it, start writing because that's where the details are clearest.

Writing Exercise Four

Freewrite on something you observed, heard, or experienced that made you feel emotional or unsettled. Describe the situation without interpretation, reproducing conversations, dialogue, and your surroundings. Then write a page, quickly, recording all your emotional responses. Choose one sentence from that page that is the emotional core and weave it into your first freewrite.

CULTURAL LOGIC: SPACE

Streets crammed with people. A human river of devoted pilgrims. Your sense of space will be challenged as you travel. On buses, in lines at the bank, at concerts—how close you sit or stand to someone, whether you push ahead in line or join diners at a table—these actions can get you into trouble or reveal your savvy. Growing up, we imbibe the cultural logic of space the way we learn language— through everyday use. It takes time to figure out these rules and how to adapt to them.

Imagine you're in Mexico traveling via Volkswagen *combi*, the ubiquitous public minivans popular throughout the country. Unlike the comfortable national buses, *combis* often squeeze twenty people into a space meant for ten. Just when the bus seems close to teetering over, someone boards with bundles of recently cut hay or a bushel of mangoes. You might fight claustrophobia as regular passengers sit undisturbed, calling out "buenas tardes" to each new person. More than anything, you want to be your ideal self, an endlessly adaptable lard-eating Traveler, completely at home on crammed *combis*. It's hard to face our own limitations. We want to remain unfazed by different notions of space and other possible discomfort. But we need to record the truth of our experiences in order to know who we are and how we change. In telling those truths, we connect to readers.

THE SLIPPERY NATURE OF TIME

The longer we spend with people, the better we understand their sense of time. But even a short stay will teach you how to negotiate daily life. You might show up for a social event at the appointed hour in many parts of Latin America, only to wait an hour for other guests to arrive. Contrast the famous punctuality of Germans and their trains. These generalizations easily slip into stereotypes. Some Latin Americans will be more prompt than some Germans. Learn the patterns but be wary of overgeneralizing.

Beyond practicalities, conceptions of time permeate life in more complex ways. In the West, time is tangible, linear, and divided into hours, days, and minutes. But before the industrial revolution, few clocks had minute hands. Writer Matt Hackett notes: "Until the 1840s, time was local and highly variable. Each town set its own clock, from which private clocks would be roughly set by hand. The time in Pittsburg [*sic*] might be 27 minutes earlier than that in New York and no one much cared."[18] The creation of the railroads demanded more uniform clocks, while World War I made wristwatches commonplace to coordinate military personnel.

How we think about time announces our values. Some cultures are famous for relaxed attitudes. Not the United States. We move ahead quickly, fixed on the future. But even in the United States, we shift into relaxed "preindustrial time" as we wander the neighborhood chatting with neighbors. Many places in the world still function in the mode of the preindustrial West; others simply perceive time differently.

Artist and researcher Sonja Dahl describes a concept central to intellectual and artistic life in Indonesia, especially in student-dominated cities such as Yogyakarta. *Nongkrong*, a friend tells her, is not just hanging out. The term points to an existential process that transcends its literal meanings—"squatting by the side of the road with a cigarette" or "sitting around because you're not doing any work." *Nongkrong*, he says, is all of these and more. Dahl explores how *nongkrong* supports collaboration among artists in an indirect but essential way. They gather, they drink coffee. They talk or they don't. Maybe nothing happens. But in that collective space, a kind of productivity foreign to the Western mind happens. Rather than fixating on the end product, Dahl argues, "nongkrong offers a holistic view of art as a long-term social process."[19] Time expands and contracts, but it never bends toward the classic capitalist formulation of time equals money.

How do we write about cultural intangibles such as time? In his memoir of living in Iran, *The Garden of the Brave in War*, Terence O'Donnell recollects what he learned about time and landscape from a group of mountain tribesmen:

They had, like so many tribesmen, that look which I have only seen before in Byzantine icons and in the faces of the Aran Islanders—a kind of stunned staring, like men caught dreaming of eternity. In the case of the icons, I do not know the reason for this look—perhaps the saints saw God—but with the tribesmen and the Aran Islanders, it may be that men who all their lives have before them great unbroken sweeps of sky and land are left wide-eyed and somehow dazed.[20]

During a visit with this group in the mountains, O'Donnell takes a nap before a wood fire. He wakes and realizes that, much to his friends' disappointment, he must return to town. A gulf separates his sense of time from theirs. Note how O'Donnell relies on story rather than trying to explain or analyze:

I wanted to stay but I knew I couldn't. The *kalantar* and some of the others came up to me. The food, they said, would soon be ready, and after that, I could sleep again. I looked at their faces and at the fires and again I was tempted. But I had made certain promises. They did not say that I should break the promises, but only that I should put them off for another day. I started walking toward the Landrover. They came along with me, looking puzzled and hurt. "Why?" the *kalantar* asked. "After all there is time—time," and he motioned toward the plain, the mountains, and the sky.[21]

Writing Exercise Five

(1) Find a public space and observe how close people stand in relation to one another, how seats are arranged, and so forth. Include details of how people looked, what they wore, and everything that was part of the scene. Describe how you felt standing so close/so far away from someone. (2) Follow with a story about time. Perhaps you arrived late or someone else did. Tell the story in scene, using narration and dialogue, as O'Donnell does, without explanation.

CRAFT DISCUSSION: DESCRIPTIVE DETAIL

We tell stories through background information—exposition or summary—and through scenes that carry the reader into our experience. We'll explore this combination in chapter 5, but both rely on a central concern of this chapter: descriptive details. Francine Prose points to the "small but significant details that, brushstroke by brushstroke, paint the pictures the artists hope to portray, the strange or familiar realities of which they hope to convince us." She includes details "of landscape and nature (the facts of marine and whale biology in *Moby Dick*) . . . of fashion (the tailors' dummies in Bruno Schulz, the hospital bracelets that the customers of the loser's bar are still wearing in Denis Johnson's *Jesus' Son*)," among others.[22] Our imaginations are sparked by concrete descriptions that allow us to see (the fiery maraschino cherry), feel (the scratchy wool), taste (the briny cod), smell (the sharp plastic scent of new cars), hear (the snap of a shoe shiner's cloth). Travel can dislodge familiar modes of description. This is good. Our best writing surprises us as well as the reader.

It's hard work to keep a narrative fresh. Writing workshops famously denigrate and discourage any worn phrase as a cliché or platitude. "Platitudes are easy," writes Leslie Jamison, "because they replace the work of singular expression with the crutch of what's been said before."[23] Clichés rely on easy assumptions and familiar interpretations, obscuring more specific, complex, or accurate information. But beware of language snobbery, Jamison adds, because clichés also link us to others, expressing commonalities in human experience.

Writing Exercise Six

Choose a central image from your surroundings or an earlier freewrite: a market stall, a house, a person's face. Look at it from different angles— from above, below, at a tilt. Describe it in detail. Weed out familiar or overused descriptions. Repeat this with a group, each person writing on the same image. Then read aloud to note the differences.

REVISION

The perspective gained through time and new writing strategies will help you revise previous writing. Description can enliven your prose by exploring what something is not (negation), what it is like (simile), or what it might be in another way of thinking (metaphor). Simile stretches our vision through explicit comparison: "His arm hung like a broken branch." Metaphor does so implicitly: "His arm was a broken branch."

Revision Exercise One

Choose an earlier freewrite and revise by deleting the adjectives. If you wrote that the family dinner table was loud, cacophonous, and lively, substitute similes and metaphors. "The family dinner table was like [or was] the Long Island railway station on a Friday in August."

Revision Exercise Two

In chapter 1, you wrote down quotes from different writers regarding the place you were headed. For example, you may have noted Michael Woolf's words about Europe as "Disney's Magic Kingdom . . . and cheap red wine." Return to those quotes now and freewrite on one. Describe how your thinking has changed.

When we begin writing, it's hard to envision the final form— memoir, essay, journalism, or some hybrid? Impressions wash over us, mixing emotions with observations. Some writers shape their books to separate the personal from the historical/cultural. In *Crescent and Star: Turkey between Two Worlds*, Stephen Kinzer recounts his years in Istanbul as bureau chief for the *New York Times*. He alternates long chapters that create journalistic portraits of people, places, and politics with short personal stories set in italics. The latter are called "meze" after the small Turkish appetizer plates that precede meals or accompany drinks.

Experiment with Form—Combine Journalism and Memoir
Adapting Kinzer's device of the meze, choose a scene you've recorded in your journal. Write a short meze in the first person recording personal reactions to an event or person. Then write about the same experience without your subjective impressions and thoughts. Use the strictly observational voice of the third person.

Finding unexpected connections enlivens understanding. Gregory Bateson knew this, as evidenced in his assignment to Ernestine McHugh to match a poem and a leaf. Comparing those structures may seem like a stretch, but the search for cultural patterns urges the "breakthrough" that Carlos Fuentes describes. Sometimes that achievement exacts a price, as it did for James Baldwin in a Paris jail, reminding us of the "travail" of travel.

In documenting breakthrough, we need to celebrate the sensuous, explore the mysterious, and, sometimes, record the painful. We need first and third person voices, clear observations, and subjective reactions. McHugh's writing abounds with details of life in the Himalayas but she does not turn away from emotion. She ends with reflections on the first words of her host mother, Lalita—"I'll be your mother." McHugh writes, "What a burden of responsibility; what a risk. What a gift it was to me, who came to her so filled with pain and hope. What she left me with was more pain and hope; the pain of knowing and loving, the hope of knowing and loving, the inevitable reality of loss."[24] To have known a culture well enough to feel such loss is the greatest gift.

3

—

ENCOUNTERING ANOTHER LANGUAGE IN YOUR OWN VOICE

In 2010, after two decades of travel and research, Ian Frazier published *Travels in Siberia*, the story of his multiple journeys over many years across one of the planet's most inhospitable territories. His story centers on his struggle to learn Russian. A quarter of the way into the book he confesses that he never fully succeeded. Frazier offers many reasons why. English speakers, for instance, have particular trouble with Russian sounds, like the Russian letter, *bI,* which is akin to the English letter *y*, but requires physical exertion. "I had to sit down hard in a chair to pronounce it," he writes.[1]

Frazier began learning the language in middle age when, as he puts it, "a grown up's dignity stumbles on the preschool mnemonics."[2] Learning Russian, in other words, involved humiliation, as learning any new language does. Frazier's story is more interesting, and his own character more endearing, because of the way he threads his labors with the language through the whole narrative, stumbling across the countryside in fractured Russian. He even takes on big novels by Tolstoy and poetry by Pushkin—in the original language. Throughout, he pokes fun at himself as he investigates a region that is as hard for him to fathom as the Russian language.

Learning a new language at any age involves modesty, humor, and a willingness to challenge routine assumptions as you wander blindly into new words and social experiences. Like Frazier, you might not understand everything. In the beginning, you might not understand much at all. Travel writer Frank Bures gets it right in his essay, "How Do You Say": "Words in other languages are like icebergs," he says. "The basic meaning is visible above the surface, but we can only guess at the shape of the vast chambers of meaning below."[3]

You'll need to map out those "chambers of meaning" to chart your own story of discovery. Use your travel journal to develop lists of words, phrases, grammatical constructions, and slang. Copy phrases from newspapers to record idioms and word usage, then practice the new vocabulary in sentences. Make notes of anecdotes, scenes, and dialogue you overheard or in which you participated. The journal will help you develop material for the writing exercises in this and other chapters and, later, to uncover rules for language.

RECORDING THE WINDING PATH
OF LANGUAGE LEARNING

Frank Bures once stumbled on one of those chambers of meaning in Tanzania. After dinner at the home of his friend Paolo one evening, his host offered to "escort" him from the house. Bures declined. "I enjoyed walking by myself," he wrote. "But I didn't realize how much had been lost in translation between Paolo's chosen English word, 'escort,' and the Swahili word for what he meant."[4] The Swahili *kusindikiza*, to accompany someone or see them off, expressed friendship and respect in a way quite different than "to escort."

Bures's example illuminates a common mistake—to misunderstand or mistranslate an expression or gesture. We all do so, and may want to immediately erase these actions from memory. But we learn the most from observing and recording the learning process, humiliations and all. Misunderstandings happen to even seasoned travelers and writers. The novelist and travel writer Paul Theroux, in a memoir of his difficult friendship with the writer V. S. Naipaul, wrote about Naipaul's attempt to learn Swahili when the two men first met in Uganda in the 1960s. "He found Swahili unpronounceable," Theroux wrote, "and was especially lost in nasalizing sounds, as when a consonant, following the rule of all Bantu languages, was softened or rubbed down by an initial *m* or *n*."[5]

Most of us can empathize more easily with Naipaul's struggles than with Theroux's mastery of foreign languages. He speaks not just Swahili but also German, Italian, and French. Yet even Theroux in a 2013 radio interview confessed his inability to pick up Portuguese on a trip to Brazil. "I couldn't get my mouth around it," he said.[6] Both writers have shown that difficult travel and language experiences provide fodder for great writing.

Writing Exercise One

Write a few pages recording a particularly difficult language-learning situation. Use scenes and dialogue to recapture the events. Then add a reflective voice: What did you learn from it?

Sometimes, the chambers of language house symbolic meaning. In French, *vache*, the word for cow, has broad metaphoric and cultural significance. Imagine you're in a hot, crowded Paris underground Metro station in July, sweat trickling down your neck when you hear someone say, "Ha! il fait vachement chaud!" This translates literally to "It's cowly hot!" or "It's hot like a cow!"

The cow simile/metaphor for intense heat actually refers to much more. In French, the cow represents something extreme in size or feeling, just as the pig in American culture is a metaphor for gross size or consumption. Consider our related phrase "to sweat like a pig." Such expressions can seem odd, since pigs don't sweat. But metaphors and similes are seldom perfectly logical.

Pushing the idea further, you can describe someone who is over-the-top angry by saying, "Il a mangé de la vache enragée"—"He ate an enraged cow." In English we have a similar expression for anger: He was so mad he had a cow. In French, though, the cow reveals deep connections between language, culture, and history. For generations before and after the industrial revolution, the cow was and remains a critical source of life in France. The milk, butter, and cheese made from a single animal's milk helped feed an entire family. As you study French history and food, you come to understand the importance of the cow on the cultural landscape, connecting people's daily lives to emotions, weather, the economy, and the largesse of food.

In any country food is central to life. Restaurants, coffee shops, or train and bus stations (where people sometimes bring their own food) invite eavesdropping and language practice. Following Ian Frazier's lead, try the next exercise.

Writing Exercise Two

Sit in a public place where people eat. Record the dialogue around you. Try to capture the idiosyncrasies of language, things akin to the role the cow plays in French. Note patterns in phrasing, intonation, or body language. Choose another set of people, another dialogue, and continue. Revise your notes and write a scene about this encounter with language.

CONNECTING LANGUAGE AND CULTURE

Imagine someone embarked on cultural study among the Dani people of western New Guinea. There, colors that North Americans or Western Europeans think of as distinct—blue versus green, for example—are lumped together in the local language. The sky and trees are *mili*, the term for dark/cool shades, while *mola* is the word for light/warm colors such as red, yellow, and white. What does that mean for how and what people see? The ways diverse societies carve up the color spectrum fascinates linguists, historians, and anthropologists. According to some scholars, our eyes first register color and then we name what we see within the boundaries of basic categories. Or is it the other way around? Do we learn language and then perceive the sky as blue, a poppy as bright red? This is the argument of the Sapir-Whorf hypothesis—a century-old linguistics theory about how language shapes cultural perception. That hypothesis has been challenged as too rigid, a kind of "linguistic determinism," but it prompts important questions about language and perspective.

Try to open yourself to the uniqueness of the language and its speakers, as many travelers have done. Charles Darwin found the clucking sounds of the people of Tierra del Fuego strange yet he also praised their skilled mimicry and sharp memories. "They could repeat with perfect correctness each word in any sentence we addressed them, and they remembered such words for some time. Yet we Europeans know how difficult it is to distinguish apart the sounds in a foreign language. Which of us, for instance, could follow an American Indian through a sentence of more than three words?"[7]

Kinship studies and terms, central to anthropology since the nineteenth century, offer a compelling entry point. How we organize and think about family influences who marries whom and what we owe one another economically and emotionally. In Hawaiian kinship, all of a parent's generation is known as "mother" on the maternal side, "father" on the paternal. In the next generation, all cousins are either "brother" or "sister." How do "sisters" behave in such a culture in contrast with, say, how you think of "sisterhood" in your own society? While kinship systems that early anthropologists encountered may seem more exotic, contemporary societies offer their own fascinating patterns: the "blended families" of remarriages; LGBT families; groups that live together in family-like settings such as communes or religious communities.

✔

Fieldwork Exercise One

In this new culture, write down the terms people use for one another in families or family-like settings. Note how people act toward those they see as "kin." Interview someone about his or her views of family. What are their responsibilities to each other?

As with family, gender patterns in language are not universal, nor are they unchanging. Many sociolinguists investigate language as "performed" in everyday life, depending on circumstances and social relations. Ways of speaking among the powerful are often more highly valued. Deborah Tannen's *You Just Don't Understand* (1994), a best-selling if now disputed book, popularized discussions of gender differences in language use in the United States.[8] Janet Holmes and Miriam Meyerhoff, writing in *The Handbook of Language and Gender* (2003), offer an overview of more culturally varied and contextual studies. Each complicates the questions: How does gendered language differ in institutional settings versus the home? How do fluid gender identity and language use challenge a binary model for understanding sociolinguistics? How do cultural differences change the discussion?[9]

After you've looked carefully at another language, reflect back on your own. In North American English, how did the word "random" evolve over the past twenty years? It's now used to emphasize something that is especially—according to urbandictionary .com—strange or crazy. Or ponder the rise of "like" in the United States. When did it start? Is it gender influenced? In linguistics, one use of "like" is to introduce a quotation ("He was, like, 'Why don't you leave now?'"). Can you suspend judgment on your own culture's language use or does "like" drive you crazy?

In chapter 7, we'll look at politics and power relations. For now, focus on recording language around you. You may cringe at the tendency for one group to dominate conversation, but you need to learn the linguistic rules before you judge.

Fieldwork Exercise Two

Venture out into different social settings, some that mix genders (perhaps a local community meeting), and others that are single gender (some beauty salons or barber shops). You might consult with someone who doesn't identity with any single category. Keep a faithful record of phrases you hear. Note body language and setting, as well as who speaks first in mixed settings, who tells jokes, and other aspects of social context.

PROVERBS, SLANG, AND OTHER LINGUISTIC BYWAYS

In *Dreaming in Chinese: Mandarin Lessons in Life, Love, and Language*, writer Deborah Fallows recounts how the language reveals "very Chinese" aspects of the country she encountered every day while living and traveling with her family. The language helped her comprehend "how people made their livings, their habits, their behavior toward each other, how they dealt with adversity and how they celebrated."[10] She recorded actions Americans might consider rude, such as shouting in closed public places. But in China, it's fine to shout "Waitress! Waitress!" in a crowded restaurant or "Off the car!" when jostling for position in the subway during rush hour. Fallows chose the language—its syntax and semantics, grammar rules and history—as her way into Chinese life, as opposed to studying art, architecture, sports, or geography. She explains that the Chinese hold their language in the highest regard: "Everyone has made a lifelong effort to learn the characters and then maintain a working command of them, so the language and its complications are always on their minds. They both goof around with the language and fear it for its superstitious power."[11]

Fallows suggests that proverbs and slang can unlock cultural meaning. Such forms fill everyday speech and literature, often embodying regional styles. Consider how often you hear in English, "Time is money" or "Don't put the cart before the horse." Language changes as each successive generation seizes on certain expressions, while changing or rejecting others. Aphorisms and adages reveal cultural and historical connections.

In his research for *Riding the Demon*, Peter recorded this example:

In Niger and Nigeria the Hausa call the [Peugeot] 504 *korea mutuwa*—calabash of death. I blinked at such a moniker for an ordinary car. There is an even more gruesome proverb for the car: *Dufa dukka kasha bakwe kibar biyu sheda*—Cook them all, kill seven, and leave two to testify or, in truncated form, *Dufa dukka*—Cook them all. The cabin seats seven passengers in three rows, but drivers add more people across the front and middle seat.[12]

In chapter 1, we suggested researching literary genres before you arrive in a place. In some cultures, oral traditions may be as important as any written forms. In every society, there are guardians of such traditions.

Fieldwork Exercise Three

Find someone who knows proverbs and traditional phrases. Record an interview about the expressions and their meaning. Follow up by asking others for their interpretations. Research the historical basis and use of such phrases. Why are they preserved and by whom? Are there regional differences in use? Follow this by charting connections between key expressions in the language and some aspect of the country.

TAKING THE LEAP: LANGUAGE IMMERSION
AND TELLING YOUR STORY

To gather material for his book on Siberia, Ian Frazier had to immerse himself in a region where very few spoke English. Joining
Russian speakers in familiar rituals and pastimes helped him learn.
A lifelong fly fisherman, Frazier seized on the sport as one avenue into the language and ways of Siberia. One day Frazier and
his friend Ivan chatted in Russian as they fished on the Chukotka
Peninsula, casting into the Bering Sea across the strait from Alaska.
"Whole five-minute periods went by," Frazier writes, "during
which I understood nothing he said."[13] It's a funny observation,
but those times of incomprehension surely led to moments of understanding. They also illustrate another seemingly magical dimension of language learning—how we pick up meaning through
expressions other than speech.

Immersion in a new culture can help you discover fresh dimensions of your own language. When Joanne lived in Northern Ireland, she wrote a daily log of street speech, gradually understanding the importance of how the letter *h* was pronounced. Take the
word "humble." A voiced *h* as in "haitch" marked you as Catholic.
But if you dropped the *h* sound for "umble," you'd be identified as
Protestant. The wrong usage in the wrong place could be dangerous. Peter lived three years in Pennsylvania as a graduate student
before he realized that people in central and western Pennsylvania
say "You'uns" rather than "you are" or "are you" when speaking
collectively of you and other people, as in: "You'uns going to the
football game on Sunday?" When you hear something new in your
own language, it helps to research the context. "You'uns," Peter
learned, is rooted in speech patterns of Scotch-Irish immigrants to
the United States and is common throughout Appalachia.

A good example of a writer juggling multiple languages in an
immersion situation is Sarah Erdman's Peace Corps memoir, *Nine
Hills to Nambonkaha: Two Years in the Heart of an African Village*, about
her time as a health worker in Côte d'Ivoire. Erdman weaves French

and two African languages, Dioula and Niarafolo, into every page of the narrative. This technique gives the reader a sense of what it's like to live in Côte d'Ivoire among speakers of numerous languages. French, the country's colonial lingua franca, works as a linguistic bridge between ethnic groups. In some cases Erdman translates, though often she leaves the reader to work it out, hoping context will clarify meaning. At the end of the book she includes a helpful glossary of common terms from all three languages.

Writing Exercise Three

Interview someone you don't know who speaks your native tongue as a second language about any topic. Take notes, listen, and observe. Make a list of new terms, note body language, and ways of speaking. Can you pick up anything new about your own language? Write a scene that captures the interview encounter.

Travelers unable or unwilling to learn new languages usually miss essential cues for how to interpret cultural meaning. Yet there are occasional examples of positive outcomes from those failures. Consider the journals of Meriwether Lewis and William Clark's journey to the Northwest in 1804–6, which detailed the landscape and indigenous peoples of the West. Lewis and Clark's mission rested on the establishment of the land as "empty" of human inhabitants, redefining the notion of frontier. Until that time, writes Peter Whitfield, "frontier" meant a line between two nations. But for the United States to stretch across the continent, that meaning had to shift to signify "the line dividing civilisation from its opposite, from emptiness, wilderness, and savagery."[14] The expedition relied heavily on Sacagawea, the now well-known Shoshoni translator. Ironically, her presence and importance signaled that, in fact, "this new territory was not empty when the Lewis and Clark party explored it."[15]

We encourage you to study and master new languages, but also to read about the language learning of travelers throughout history.

GRAFFITI AND OTHER FORMS
OF VISUAL LANGUAGE

Visual language awakens us in different ways than the spoken word. All cultures communicate through symbols and icons. A nation's flag is a good example. We also use body language, facial expressions, and clothing—elements Ian Frazier likely relied on as the Russian words of his fishing companion passed right over him. There are so many ways to "speak" without verbal language.

Visual signposts that combine word and image are everywhere: on street names and other place markers, on the sides of walls, the back of trucks and cars, on billboards. Political sloganeering, bumper stickers, and other kinds of language all invite cultural interpretation. Think of the way advertising works through images. You may remember the Marlboro Man, the iconic "strong and silent" horseman of a bygone era. Philip Morris and Company shaped the image to promote their new filter cigarettes, which had previously been seen as "feminine." You may find opportunities for excavating commercial or political agendas behind advertisements as you travel and live abroad.

In our hometowns, we often ignore or don't know the origins or significance of street and place names. Names connect to history, while renaming exhibits political shifts. Consider how many streets in U.S. cities are now named for Martin Luther King Jr. In Mexico, many cities have a calle 20 de noviembre, a date critical to the revolution, and one marking independence day, 16 de septiembre. Most Mexicans can tell you the meaning of these dates. But other streets commemorate historic figures with complex histories. Bartolomé de las Casas was a sixteenth-century Dominican friar and reformer who worked on behalf of indigenous people but he's also been criticized for supporting the African slave trade (a view he later renounced). Some residents would recount both views of de las Casas; others would not. Interviews and research can disclose such complexity.

☑

Fieldwork Exercise Three

Choose a specific neighborhood and make a chart of streets and other place names. Ask at least three different people to explain the gist of each. Can they tell stories about the historic figures or events? Have some street and/or place names changed?

As preparation for traveling, you researched the arts and architecture of this new place; by now, you may have ventured into museums or galleries or onto the street. Art as a specialized realm divorced from daily life dates back just a few centuries. Contemporary Western institutions distinguish crafts people, artisans, and folk or traditional artists from their "fine art" counterparts. But in smaller communities and throughout much of the world, art is fused with daily life. Traditional arts may be utilitarian but aesthetically important, like the Japanese baskets Alison Buckholtz so coveted (see chapter 1). Sometimes visual arts mix with oral tradition and religious practices in rituals of celebration and healing. The divisions shift; art can change location and thus shift perception. Think about American quilts, a folk art that feminists moved from beds to galleries in the 1970s.

Perhaps you're focused on graffiti, which has been around for millennia. In the eighteenth century, names and bawdy messages were discovered under the Roman walls of Pompeii. "Tagging" grew in 1970s New York and then London, moving uptown to galleries in the 1990s. Now such art is mainstream in many quarters, commercialized by figures like the mysterious Banksy, whose reprints are sold on the Internet. The late Jean-Michel Basquiat got his start in New York as a graffiti artist before his paintings became an international sensation.

Art may challenge dominant interpretations of symbols and events. Examples include political posters such as "No Blood for

Oil" at the outbreak of the Iraq war in 2003 or the murals covering Belfast walls that depict Catholic versus Protestant versions of
history. Street arts abound in cities, offering another vision of cultural aesthetics. Consider, on that score, work such as Soraya Mo-
rayef's website about Egyptian street art (https://suzeeinthecity
.wordpress.com/).

Fieldwork Exercise Four

Walk the streets and take photos of graffiti and other forms of public
art. Interview people about specific pieces: is that carved wooden fish on
someone's lawn considered art? What about a handwoven shawl a woman
wears on the street in Peru? Does its status change when exported to a
Cusco gallery's wall? Finally, find a library or archival source where you
can further research what you've discovered.

REVERSING THE GAZE

In chapter 1, we encouraged reading about how people from
other countries view the United States or whatever country you
might call home. We cited Margaret Atwood's humorous critique of Americans. In *Portraits of "the Whiteman,"* anthropologist
Keith Basso offers a perspective based on his linguistic research—a
Western Apache view of whites. One "joking performance" by an
Apache is set in a bar, with J, a cowboy, welcoming L, an "Indian
friend." J slaps L on the shoulder, looks him directly in the eyes,
and shakes his hand wildly, saying, "Come right in, my friend!
Don't stay outside in the rain. Better you come in right now . . . Sit
down! Sit right down! Take your loads off you [*sic*] ass. You hungry? You want some beer? Maybe you want some wine? You want
crackers? . . . You sure looking good to me, L. You looking pretty
fat! Pretty good all right!"[16]

The verbal assault goes on in hilarious fashion, each additional exclamation a further breach of Apache etiquette. For one needs to know, as Basso does from his years of study, that the Apache would never use "my friend." The closest equivalent word in Apache means "toward me, he is good." Close relationships are forged through time. As one Apache told Basso, "White men say you're their friend like it was nothing, like it was air."[17] An Apache would not ask how another person is feeling or physically touch someone in public. The entire performance brims with unacceptable behavior, which is of course why the Apache find it so entertaining.

The examples you encounter may be subtler but humor is a great teacher. Often, joke tellers can't say why something is amusing. As Freud knew, and any stand-up comedian can affirm, humor reveals its meanings sideways.

Consider another example where word and image meet: political cartoons. Caricature and cultural background combine to make cartoons work. Context is key, so cultural outsiders are often befuddled until they understand what the cartoon alludes to. If you can access newspapers with cartoons, explore this important aspect of culture.

Fieldwork Exercise Four
Talk to people you meet to find out what comedy shows are popular, visit a club, or read political cartoons in the newspaper. Write down jokes or skits. Interview residents about a particular joke and ask them to explain the humor.

CRAFT DISCUSSION: DEVELOPING THE WRITER'S VOICE

Voice connects to point of view, which we discuss again in chapter 9 on revision. Point of view is the way a story is told, that is, in first person ("I" or "we"), second person, ("you"), or third person ("she," "he," "they"). Each offers unique strengths. The "I" claims authority for the writer. "We" establishes a collective sensibility. "You" pulls the reader into a scene, sometimes doing double duty as the writer speaking to him- or herself and to the reader. "A strong, well-executed point of view will also lead to a strong voice," argues writer and editor Lee Gutkind.[18]

Different media have particular voices. Newspapers, for example, often feature a crisp and direct, fast-paced tone dependent on short paragraphs and sentences. Literary journalism offers other, contrasting styles, often using the first person in ways traditional journalists frown on. As we've noted, the first person "I" does not mean that the story is about you; rather, your immersion in a setting allows for transmission of the story. Think of your first-person narrative voice as a camera lens. Even in first person, remember to hover in the background to make the witnessing self less apparent. "The cardinal rule," Paul Theroux said about travel writing, "is to be as unobtrusive as possible."[19]

Another way to understand voice is as the distinctive personality or attitude that rises from the writing on the page. Learning to develop that voice is one of the most confounding problems facing a writer. The statement "I'm trying to develop my voice in this essay" is about as clear as saying, "I'm going off to try and find myself." Still, good writers create voice through practice and concrete tools: syntax, diction, and development of narrative structure, dialogue, setting, and character. Maybe it helps to think of this line from F. Scott Fitzgerald's *The Great Gatsby*: "The exhilarating ripple of her voice was a wild tonic in the rain."[20] This is the voice of . . . a man in love?

Look at the opposing voices of two fiction writers, Ernest Hemingway and James Joyce. Hemingway, who began his career as a journalist, wrote in a style often described as "minimalist" or "crisp" or "punchy" for the way he used short, tight sentences. Hemingway's famously rapid-fire dialogue sometimes runs down one side of a page, as in his novel *A Farewell to Arms*. James Joyce is sometimes described as a "purple" writer whose work is less controlled—some say "uncontrolled." *Ulysses* is famous for sentences that go on for pages. Both writers have a vivid, visual writing style, which is part of what makes them still relevant today.

In nonfiction, consider what Joan Didion, also a journalist and novelist, achieves in the first paragraph of her essay, "Some Dreamers of the Golden Dream," about an unusual murder case. She writes:

The San Bernardino Valley lies only an hour east of Los Angeles by the San Bernardino Freeway but it is in certain ways an alien space: not the coastal California of the subtropical twilights and the soft westerlies off the Pacific but a harsher California, haunted by the Mojave just beyond the mountains, devastated by the hot dry Santa Ana wind that comes down through the passes at 100 miles an hour and whines through the eucalyptus windbreaks and works on the nerves.[21]

In one sentence Didion builds the character of a specific California setting in a way now considered uniquely hers. The sentence might be viewed as a run-on. But notice how Didion employs active verbs—"haunted," "devastated," "comes," "whines," "works"—in an overly long sentence that manages, by its own winding length and spare punctuation, to mimic the way the Santa Ana wind moves. Didion is well known for using the language this way, just as the playwright David Mamet is famous for his sharp and fast dialogue.

One way to develop your own style is to imitate writers whose work you admire. In *The Sincerest Form*, Nicholas Delbanco writes that "imitation is the route to authenticity."[22] He suggests young writers practice adopting the style of three or four different writers. Learning from their stylistic successes and failures, he argues, will develop a sharper sense of your own voice. You pick up the writing tics you find helpful and discard the rest.

While voice is decidedly individual, it also reflects cultural influences in language. The very British "bit warm today, isn't it?" contrasts with the casual U.S. "warm enough for ya?" We need to avoid stereotypes yet still stay alert to subtle and revealing uses of language.

Has learning another language sharpened your sensitivity to language in general? Do you see this in your writing?

Writing Exercise Five

Set aside a sample of your writing and examine your own style. Read it aloud, slowly. Make some notes about quirks that you believe reflect your own voice. Are you aware of specific habits or ways of creating sentences, using verbs, or describing character and landscape?

REVISION

Now that you've delved deep into how language connects to people's lives, and identified aspects of your own voice, you can revise previous work to reflect that learning.

Revision Exercise One

Choose a piece of writing from your journal or an essay you think is finished. Revise a few pages of it in the voice and style of a writer you admire. Do this three times, choosing a different "model" writer every time. Is there a particular style that feels more comfortable? As we noted in chapter 1, when you "borrow" another writer's structure, you need to acknowledge the source of your inspiration.

Revision Exercise Two

Take that same writing and change generic terms to specific ones (not "tree" but "maple" or "madrona"). Use local names for streets, people, and places even if they are in a language the reader may not know. Specifics add precision, clarity, and cultural depth and build a reader's trust in you as a knowledgeable guide. Your voice also gains strength and authority.

Revision often involves expanding and combining freewrites to search for a form. Other times, you might begin with a specific structure and weave material into that form. Below are possible ways to create a structure.

Revision Exercise Three

Reread the freewrites in this chapter. Find at least two or three that connect. Read them aloud to yourself or a partner. Makes notes on recurrent themes and threads. Underline lines or phrases that you want to expand. Start a new freewrite with one of those and add it to your piece. Create a rough draft, doing more writing as you go.

Experiment with Form—Try a Lyric Essay

Lyric essay is a form poised between poetry and prose. It relies on putting fragments together or finding a refrain to structure the piece. Make a list of phrases in a new language taken from your freewrites. Tell a story for each phrase, perhaps where you encountered it, what you learned, and from whom. Keep each story to about 250 words and then put them into a mosaic, each short segment set off by a line break with only loose or even no formal transitions.

WHAT LANGUAGE UNLOCKS

Even if you don't master another language, the attempt opens unique cultural pathways. Ian Frazier never realized his dream of mastering Russian. In 2005, after fifteen years of studying and exploring everything related to Siberia, Frazier took another Russian course from the same instructor who told him he spoke "hooligan Russian."[23] At the end, the teacher administered the verbal exam the U.S. State Department requires of its diplomats. Frazier earned a grade of 2+, rating him as barely conversational. He compares his struggles to speak and understand Russian to "using a telephone with a bad connection."[24] But Frazier's endeavors enriched his understanding of Siberia and his writing. His readers gained new vision about a part of the world alternately demonized and embraced by the United States, and one frequently subject to stereotypes.

The eighteenth-century German writer and statesman, Johann Goethe, reminds us that learning other languages always returns us homeward. In his philosophical meditation, *Maxims and Reflections*, he wrote, "A man who has no acquaintance with foreign languages knows nothing of his own."[25] The words of American novelist and Nobel laureate Toni Morrison deepen the meaning of Goethe's reflection: "We die. That may be the meaning of life. But we do language. That may be the measure of our lives."[26]

4

DOCUMENTARY FORMS

AND METHODS

In 1936, James Agee accepted an assignment from *Fortune Magazine* to write about rural tenant farmers in the American South. He likely didn't realize how much pain he would confront—in the Alabama farmers' lives or in his own heart. He never finished the magazine piece but did eventually publish *Let Us Now Praise Famous Men*—an unruly and unclassifiable work. The book brims with Agee's uncertainty about his goals and laments about the limitations of words. "If I could do it," Agee wrote, "I'd do no writing at all here. It would be photographs; the rest would be fragments of cloth, bits of cotton, lumps of earth, records of speech, pieces of wood and iron, phials of odors, plates of food and of excrement."[1]

In the final book, photos did accompany Agee's text—the now iconic images produced by Walker Evans, his companion on the journey. But his misgivings speak to broader issues, questions that continue to haunt those exploring culture: What drives us to document the lives of others, and what artistic tools best shape that record? Are words, in fact, inadequate? Would Agee have been better served by a video camera to reproduce those fragments? Certainly, we'd now have a different vision of the farmers' lives. But we'd also sacrifice a classic work that has inspired documentarians for decades. In fact, twenty-first-century technologies might not have soothed Agee's anguish. Central Alabama was Agee's "abroad" and he had to grapple with his dilemmas as a writer, as we all must.

Bouncing along in a rickshaw in Delhi, perhaps you're facing your own decisions. You're awash in the bright pink of saris worn by passing women, the orange and crimson of fruit in vendors' stalls, deafened by honking horns, animal and human cries. An idea takes shape and you dig in your bag for your notebook. Perhaps you'll regret losing the flow of image and sound around you. Or you let the writing idea go and reach instead for the camera or recorder. Maybe you'll mourn that lost thought or maybe it will reemerge from the image you glean. Other forms enrich and accompany words to preserve what we witness in our travels, the pain as well as the joy—what James Agee called "the cruel radiance of what is."[2]

"Documentary" comes from the literal meaning of the term— "factual, meant to provide a record." Add to that the personal passion of the documentarian. The result melds subjectivity and observation, art and social science. Documentary today includes writing, photography, audio postcards and programs, oral histories, digital stories, and film. Travel and cultural exploration invite these combinations as we record and transform our experiences. Writer, psychiatrist, and documentary writer and teacher Robert Coles speaks to how this work relates to travel: "Doing documentary work is a journey, and is a little more, too . . . a passage that can become a quest, even a pilgrimage, a movement toward the sacred truth enshrined not only on tablets of stone, but in the living hearts of those whom we can hear, see, and get to understand."[3]

All media rely on story. As writer Duncan Murrell asserts, "The first task of the documentary writer is discovery and documentation, the second task is form. The documentary writing process is fundamentally open to integration of other media, but the story itself always dictates the form. Documentary writers think of themselves as storytellers first, writers/filmmakers/photographers/ recorders second."[4] Each form demands conscientious attention to detail—the daily record of where and when images were taken. Each poses ethical questions about the rights of people whose lives are documented. The rootedness in "factual" and "record" remains as essential as the imaginative shaping of a narrative.

ILLUSTRATION AND IMAGE

Before photography, travelers represented their experiences with ink, paint, and dedicated attention. Historical examples include the Victorian artist David Roberts. His drawings of people and architectural sites in Syria, Egypt, and other parts of the Middle East created new images for Europeans. These depictions are important despite their "orientalist" view of Arab cultures as backwards but exotic and mysterious.

Artists today continue to register impressions in travel journals online and in notebooks that pair word and image. The sketches, writing, and painting of Candace Rose are one example of this (http://www.candaceroserardon.com/). Her work and that of many others urge us to slow down and train the eye to see differently than we do when we frame a photograph.

Not all of us are gifted sketchers or painters, but most people now carry a camera. Photographs became part of travelers' accounts in the nineteenth century when sojourners abroad introduced slides into their presentations. John Lawson Stoddard was a New England teacher who realized a lifelong dream when he began to travel in 1874, returning with stories that became books. But he also incorporated slide transparencies of historic scenes, photos, engravings, and other visuals that made his public lectures hugely popular.

As with travel writing, photos reflect the attitudes of each historical period. "Pictorialism," which dominated late nineteenth-century photography, colored and softened images in response to critiques that photos were mere reproductions of reality, not a true art form. In twentieth-century America, photographers turned a sharp focus to life as lived on the street and in the world—James Agee's "cruel radiance." Photographer and writer Gretchen Garner calls this approach "spontaneous witness"—a method and vision still central to photojournalists and documentarians. Now, post-modern collage, photography about photography, and other styles add to a medley of approaches.[5]

Watch a woman pose for a selfie against the Great Wall of China. Consider a group of friends clowning for a shot next to a pyramid. Smart phones and tablets as well as traditional cameras are everywhere. We're also bombarded by contemporary and historical images of a place before we get there. You might carry to Ho Chi Minh City the widely viewed photo of a nine-year-old girl, Phan Thị Kim Phúc, fleeing the village of Trang Bang after a napalm attack during the Vietnam War. Some photos, despite overdisplay, don't lose their power. Others are hackneyed from endless replay on YouTube or social media sites. Television and movies, digital images and the Internet, have intensified the dangers of sentimentalizing or exoticizing another culture. We prompt the "exotic" when we show difference without the hard-earned understanding of context. The sentimental takes over, said documentary photographer Dorothea Lange, when someone creates "a rehash of a rehash of a rehash of something that wasn't very deeply grounded at the beginning," triggering "shallow emotionalism."[6] Our goal is to awaken new vision through images as well as words.

Photographs can illustrate your stories and stimulate memory, like visual journal entries. But ethical practices and forethought are essential. This is tricky, as compelling images often rely on split-second response. But taking a picture may invade someone's privacy or undermine the subject's dignity. People may resent having their photographs taken without permission for religious or cultural as well as personal reasons. Power relations matter. Children and people with less economic or other forms of power may be afraid to object even if they don't want to be photographed.

Many professional photographers take close-up photos only with the subject's permission. Some seek written consent if they are going to use the photo for a specific online or print publication. Others, particularly when covering breaking news stories, are more aggressive. Street shots taken from a distance usually don't require permission; however, this depends on the place and cultural rules. In Europe, particularly France and Germany, privacy safeguards are far more stringent than in the United States. An individual's dignity may matter more than the public's right to news. This happened in France following the 2015 Paris terrorist attacks. A French photographer who raced to the Bataclan concert hall faced a legal case when her photo of one of the victims appeared in a glossy weekly magazine.

The needs and ethics of a news photographer differ from those of a traveler or student abroad. But the National Press Photographers Association offers a baseline code of ethics at their website.[7] While these guidelines forbid payment for photographs, some travelers offer other kinds of exchange. A Paraguayan market woman selling mangoes might be happy to be photographed after you make a purchase. It's best to feel your way into each situation after researching the attitudes of the culture.

Similar cautions apply if you are recording with audio or video equipment (see below for a discussion of obtaining signed permission).

✔

Writing Exercise One

Assemble a group of your photos. Be sure to label each image in your photo program or in a separate log, noting the date, place, and names of people involved. Don't assume you'll remember. Choose one photo, and then follow this series of freewrites:

1. Write what you see without replicating what the photo shows. For example, if you photographed a young woman in a white dress, don't tell us this is a young woman in a white dress. Tell us, instead, that

this is an almost fifteen-year-old getting ready for her *quinceañera*, a coming-of-age celebration in Mexico.

2. Write about what you feel when you look at this image.
3. Write about what you imagine the subject is thinking or feeling. Make it clear to the reader that you are speculating. Begin with, "He [or she] might have been thinking/feeling . . ." or "I imagine . . ."
4. Write about what is outside the frame of this photo: temporally, what happened before and after you took the picture, and/or spatially, what physically surrounds the frame of the photo.

Both before and during your travels, research websites and print publications about documentary photography—a world so vast we couldn't hope to cover it here. One online publication that publishes photos and writing, *Cargo Literary*, echoes the goal of many travel writers—to inspire and celebrate cultural diversity as well as "personal passage" (http://cargoliterary.com/). Among the many print and online publications, such as *National Geographic*, lies a hidden gem—the beautifully produced *Double Take Magazine*, now sadly out of print. The "double" refers to the equal weight given to word and image, a balance to strive for in documentary work. Text and image can complement and sharpen one another, illuminating nuances.

The Peace Corps encourages volunteers to submit photos to the media library found at their website (http://medialibrary .peacecorps.gov/). Students on study abroad programs also post photos, often combined with other documents of their travels. Check out any university website to see the range of possibilities. One example is *Aleph*, a journal of global perspectives featuring the work of students on overseas programs from Hobart and William Smith Colleges and Union College (https://alephweb.wordpress .com/). Some organizations connect photography with activism, a topic we discuss at the end of this chapter. The Blue Earth Alliance supports "visual storytelling on critical environmental and social issues through direct assistance to photographers and a collaborative community of professionals" (http://blueearth.org/).

CAPTURING SOUND: VOICES AND INTERVIEWS

In chapter 3, we discussed the voice of the writer. In the next chapter, we'll explore how to write profiles based on the voices of others. Whether you're a journalist, traveler, ethnographer, or all three, at some point during your travels, you'll do interviews. These might be formal or informal, focused on an individual or a group. You may couple good old-fashioned note taking with use of a recording device. For written notes, use a small, unobtrusive notebook. Jot down keywords as shorthand for longer stories. Barry Lopez, describing the stories he heard in Africa, compared such keywords to "buttons" held by coiled thread. He mentally wound the story around the button; later, he unraveled the thread to re-create the full tale.

Using a recorder frees you to write notes on the person's appearance, body language, and the general environment. With an accurate account of a person's words, you're less likely to misquote. But mechanical devices can make us lazy and inattentive. They may also intimidate people, especially in cultures not used to technology (though these are becoming rare). Finally, machines can malfunction. You finish satisfied that you've got the goods only to discover a blank file later. A device that displays the record function helps but nothing is foolproof.

Alex Kotlowitz, the award-winning author of *There Are No Children Here: The Story of Two Boys Growing Up in the Other America*, only records when he's interviewing a public figure who might contest what he writes. John McPhee advocates a device but "maybe not as a first choice—more like a relief pitcher."[8] Jon Krakauer, who takes notes and records, says, "I'm like a human sponge. Anything that happens anywhere near me gets recorded, whether on paper or on tape."[9] These decisions also influence audio and video. Video may seem more intimidating to interviewees, but smart phones and other hand-held devices make this increasingly less likely.

As preparation, you should read enough about your subject to ask relevant questions. You don't want to insult someone or miss critical clues through ignorance. But both journalists and ethnographers sometimes act unaware or childlike, prompting the interviewee to expand and clarify. As John McPhee notes, only half facetiously, "Who is going to care if you seem dumber than a cardboard box? Reporters call that creative bumbling."[10]

A note on language: knowing another language well is obviously optimal for interviews. However, you can work with varying levels of fluency. Some journalists rely on translators. Adam Hochschild, while writing a book about Stalin's legacy, knew enough Russian to do his own interviews, then had a bilingual speaker transcribe them into English. This revealed wonderful material he hadn't realized he was collecting.

Styles of interviews vary. If you're pursuing a subject, say, Ramadan traditions in a Muslim community, you'll want to focus your questions. Journalists generally direct the process in this fashion. In contrast, oral historians allow narrators to hold forth on what is important to them. Your goal is to elicit stories and let the unexpected unfold. You don't want yes or no answers so aim for open-ended questions. For example, instead of "Was it difficult when the police raided your house?" ask, "What was most difficult about house raids?" Keep a list of questions handy, even if you don't refer to it. Always, listening is key.

A cautionary note on something we've discussed in other chapters: interviewers should try to suspend their point of view. Refrain from judgment, even if known facts contradict what you're hearing. Remember that people tell you *their* version of events. Italian historian Alessandro Portelli argues that oral history is not just what people did but "what they wanted to do, what they believed they were doing, and what they now think they did."[11] Oral histories can reflect social myths and beliefs that are shaped collectively through the telling and retelling of stories. We're after meaning as well as factual accounts. What we learn is partial, modified by gaps in memory, and by the social position of the storyteller as well as the interviewer.

Fieldwork Exercise One

Choose a person or persons to interview. Arrange a preinterview to establish trust and begin a relationship. Be sure to discuss your intentions and goals. At that meeting, take notes on the discussion, the setting, the person's physical appearance, and the entire context. As soon as possible, write up your notes. Follow up with library research and create questions. Following the steps outlined below, conduct a first interview. Afterwards, summarize your notes and transcribe the recording. Generate questions for a possible second interview (with or without video; see fieldwork exercise 2 below).

There are multiple and ever-changing websites and publications with practical tips for recording oral histories and other types of interviews. Here are a few:

https://www.loc.gov/folklife/edresources/edcenter_files/interview
    -guide.pdf
http://dohistory.org/on_your_own/toolkit/oralHistory.html
http://oralhistory.library.ucla.edu/interviewGuidelines.html
http://www.oralhistory.org/about/principles-and-practices/

Regardless of the type of interview, remember some basic rules: Always test a recorder in advance. Find a good location and eliminate background noise. Check recording levels during the interview. Tag the beginning of the recording by stating the date, time, location, your name, and the name of your interviewee for proper archiving and cataloging. Secure a release from the person if appropriate but be sure to carefully research the terms of agreement. In the past, when interviewees signed a release, they transferred copyright to an archives or a library that would house the material and make it available to researchers. But with widespread Internet use, many repositories now share oral histories and related material online. Release forms often need to be modified to account for possible online distribution. The Institute of Museum and Library Services' website features a provocative discussion of the politics of ownership and use of oral histories. One proposal comes from "Creative Commons," a nonprofit whose licensing tools strive to balance copyright with public access to information (http://ohda .matrix.msu.edu/2012/06/a-creative-commons-solution/).

The institute also offers a useful guide for making oral history videos, should you decide to add a visual component to the recording.[12]

INDEXING AND TRANSCRIBING

Creating an index for interviews is a useful step to help you locate material later. Start with the time code on the file set to 00:00:00 on the clock of your computer or playback device, then summarize subjects, themes, and general data. If your interview begins with a person's memory of the Cuban Revolution, you might log from 00–1:30 this way: "Describes rural life in his village; his mother's weaving work; his father's farming practices." When the topic shifts at say, a minute and thirty-two seconds, mark the time and begin a new category, using small increments to group material and make it more accessible.

Transcribing involves writing down, word for word, what you've recorded. You can eliminate "ums" and other filler and use ellipses (. . .) for material that seems extraneous. But don't make that decision too quickly. That tangent you're tempted to eliminate may prove essential. Yes, it's tedious but if you do the work yourself, you'll learn a lot about a person from his or her tone of voice, inflection, rhythm, and other aspects of speech. You'll hear the music of language. You'll also pick up content you missed during the interview. Some journalists do all their own transcription; others may do one or two transcriptions to get a sense of a subject's voice and then hire someone to complete the process. Having an exact record also lets you scan for keywords and find connections you might otherwise miss. For example, in writing *Remedios*, Joanne found metaphors in Eva Castellanoz's speech through scanning for keywords. She later used these as chapter headings to organize the book.

Some folklorists and anthropologists note the performance aspects of oral storytelling in the actual transcript. Words delivered in a louder voice, for example, may appear in capital letters, while poetic speech might be rendered in verse. Ethnopoetics, pioneered by poet Jerome Rothenberg and by folklorists and anthropologists Dell Hymes and Dennis Tedlock, recognizes the poetic quality of certain kinds of speech and performances. Ethnopoetic notation has been particularly important with Native American texts.[13]

Many transcribers note the elapsed time at specific intervals for the duration of the interview. For instance, the American Folklife Center marks the transcription every five minutes. An example from the Civil Rights History Project at the Library of Congress and the Smithsonian National Museum of African American History and Culture shows a time marker on page 8, just after "I can remember members of the Albany Movement stopping in at our church to, um, talk [15:00]."[14]

Creating a transcript, partial or total, is similar for video and audio. A guide created by the Oral History in a Digital Age Project covers both.[15]

CAPTURING SOUND: RECORDING THE ENVIRONMENT

Cultural anthropologist and writer/documentarian Richard Nelson has lived for decades in Sitka, Alaska, studying Alaska Native cultures. One of his books, *Make Prayers for the Raven: A Koyukon View of the Northern Forest*, documents an Athapaskan group's perception of the natural world—their language, landscape, subsistence cycle, and relationships to animals. In 1987, Nelson collaborated with the Koyukon and with KUAC-TV, University of Alaska—Fairbanks, to produce a series of five video episodes spanning a year of subsistence life. The project reflects the importance of collaboration in documentary work, melding sound and image to preserve unique perspectives on the natural world.[16]

Nelson's work with radio also documents sound in imaginative ways. For programs set in Alaska and Australia, he intersperses personal and cultural commentary with the sounds of animals and landscapes in his Encounters podcast (http://www.encountersnorth .org/). In one program, he shares stories of his experiences with Kookaburras and pied butcherbirds, weaving in memories of listening to Radio Australia as a child (http://encountersnorth.org/audio _files/Encounters_Kookaburra.mp3).

Sound recorders traverse the globe. Chris Watson, who has worked on many BBC documentaries, started at age eleven, registering bird cries in his yard. He's branched out to the Antarctic (the groan of ice straining), Kenya (the clamor of vultures picking apart a dead zebra), and other worlds. Closer to home in Newcastle, England, he captured the noise of an insect called the water boatman. "It's the sound of them rubbing their penises beneath their abdomens to sing to attract females," Watson explains.[17] Sound carries us to worlds we'll never experience and preserves the aural present for future generations.

What will you do with sound recordings? You might broadcast through a local radio program while you're traveling or produce a podcast for the Internet. Perhaps you made arrangements with a station at home to send back audio postcards. The following exercise will help you create a vivid oral component of the culture you're studying.

Writing Exercise Two

Choose an earlier freewrite about a place that you can return to. Go back and record the sound environment and then revise the freewrite to incorporate what you heard, perhaps using onomatopoeia to bring the sounds to life. If you're writing a blog (see chapter 8), you can add the sound clips to your site.

VISUAL DOCUMENTATION: FILM AND VIDEO

The terminology for visual documentation is a palimpsest, with previous meanings layered under changing contemporary usage. "Film" and "video" stem from their respective technologies for capturing light, but they're often used interchangeably. Audrey Amidon, a preservation specialist in the Motion Picture Preservation Lab of the National Archives, makes a useful distinction: "If you shot it on your smart phone, that's a video. If you inserted it into your VCR in 1994, it's a video. If you used a projector, which in its most basic form is a machine that moves a strip of plastic past a light source at 24 frames per second, then, yes, you do indeed have a film in your hands."[18]

Digital formats now dominate, though we still talk about feature length movies as "filmed" and the record of a speaker's lecture as "taped." Despite the lag in accurate language, what matters is learning to combine moving images, sound, and words to document cultures in meaningful and ethical ways.

Travel inspired some of the earliest films. Short travelogues called scenics were popular in early twentieth-century America. They exploited the nineteenth-century technology pioneered by the Lumière brothers—the French inventers of one the first motion picture cameras. Among inaugural documentary films was Robert Flaherty's *Nanook of the North* (1922). Though an overly simplistic and romanticized image of an Inuit hunter, the film represented a way of life then little known outside the Arctic. This critique may sound familiar. It echoes current analysis of early travel narratives that brought unfamiliar cultures to life but with distortions. No documentary form duplicates reality. Film historian Bill

Nichols points out that documentaries are "expressive representations" rather than simple reproductions.[19] As with writing, each represents a distinct point of view.

Film also figures in the history of French, British, and American ethnography, including Margaret Mead and Gregory Bateson's recording of rituals in Bali and New Guinea in the 1930s. Pioneers such as Jean Rouch influenced the development of local cinema in Niger and the other parts of Africa where he worked. Most ethnographers today include a visual component in their work, whether it's technically film or video. But in a postcolonial, technologically changing world, previously documented groups can return the gaze of the ethnographer. The insider versions of their lives may challenge the existing record. Many groups now collaborate on projects. In 1966, academic researchers Sol Worth, John Adair, and Richard Chalfen trained members of Navajo communities in Pine Springs, Arizona, to make their own films. The University of Pennsylvania Museum of Archaeology and Anthropology distributed the films under the title *Navajo Film Themselves*. These are now available as DVDs from Visionmaker, a Native American video project, with the inclusion of newly found material. In another example, Beate Engelbrecht worked with artisans in the Mexican town of Santa Clara del Cobre to produce the film, *Copper Working* (1993). The artisans used the film to promote tourism and market their work.

Some documentary filmmakers incorporate the footsteps of earlier travelers. In a remote corner of Wyoming, Ian McCluskey, the founding director of NW Documentary, happened on a plaque commemorating the 1938 kayak journey of a French trio, two of them newlyweds, down the Colorado River. Captivated, he explored their voyage and discovered journals, photographs, and 16 mm films they left behind. Seventy-five years after their original journey, he retraced their kayak voyage—a film version of immersion journalism. The film integrates his contemporary exploration with the early footage. He also visited the town in France the trio had come from and interviewed their descendants, finding unexpected connections. *Voyagers without Trace* captures the beauty of the landscape and a story of intrepid travelers and underscores the need to preserve film histories as well as treasured landscapes.

Videos shot on cameras or smart phones accompany many travel accounts, often with blogs and/or photos. The Peace Corps websites feature not only photos (mentioned above) but also award-winning videos from volunteers. A storytelling guide appears on the Peace Corps site as well. A related link gives instructions on how to create videos—useful for all kinds of travelers and students abroad.[20]

An extremely valuable tool is Nancy Kalow's *Visual Storytelling: The Digital Video Documentary*, a free publication of the Center for Documentary Studies at Duke University. Kalow, a passionate advocate for creating greater access to filmmaking, shares her "no-nonsense, inexpensive, and ethical approaches to creating documentary video."[21] Kalow also gives a valuable overview of the necessity for signed consent, particularly if you plan to show a film or video to a broader public. Her guide includes a sample permission form.

Fieldwork Exercise Two

Do another interview with the person whose oral history you recorded (see fieldwork exercise 1 above) to add a video component. You can build on questions that came up as you transcribed the first oral history. Follow-up also reveals greater depths of your subject's personality and additional insights into varied topics. Repeat the note-taking and transcription process. If you don't have access to the original subject, choose someone new for the video project, following the same preparation process.

DIGITAL STORIES

"Digital storytelling" is a broad term for multimedia built on some blend of words, photos, video clips, drawings, and other images, often accompanied by music and/or narration. Digital technologies have revolutionized storytelling in ways that pull viewers into the experience and democratize who gets to share stories, including tales of travel. A people's medium, if you will.

Digital stories are widespread in educational settings. Teachers create stories as instructional tools—critical to keep the attention of students raised in multimedia environments. Students use the technologies to relate personal experiences and document those of others. In higher education, study abroad program websites often integrate digital stories with student blogs. The video guides cited above are useful for both framing images and creating digital narratives. Music adds to the creative mix of media.

The website of Story Center, formerly the Center for Digital Storytelling, provides numerous resources and workshops, both on-site and online (http://www.storycenter.org/).

If you want to learn documentary methods before you travel, many universities as well as community centers house programs that incorporate film, video, photography, and other formats. The Duke University Center for Documentary Studies has one of the largest of these programs. Another long-standing program, the Salt Institute for Documentary Studies, is now part of Maine College of Art. The New School in New York offers a Documentary Media Studies Graduate Certificate.[22] Explore online sites and local universities or community arts centers for training opportunities.

Writing Exercise Three

Create a digital story that charts a range of your travels. Perhaps you've accumulated photos from a year in India. You might choose images from the ashram where you spent a month, life with a family in Mumbai, and hiking with a group in the Himalayas. Set up a slide show with accompanying music.

DOCUMENTARIAN AS WITNESS AND ACTIVIST

Many travelers and sojourners abroad, perhaps sharing James Agee's angst over the human suffering they encounter, merge social action with documentary work. Take the case of Emma Raynes, a Lewis Hine Documentary Fellow at the Duke Center for Documentary Studies in 2007–8. She worked with Brazilian migrant workers who must leave their families in the Jequitinhonha Valley each year for six to ten months to cut sugarcane in São Paulo. Raynes photographed the departing men and recorded their voices to create a framed image and CD for each family. Later, she helped the children shape photos and sound recordings into audiovisual "letters" to send their fathers. Raynes eventually turned the project over to local community leaders. Born of a local need, documented by an outsider, rendered in creative multimedia, the project is a compelling example of art as social practice in an interconnected world (http://documentarystudies.duke.edu/projects/emma-raynes-pai -estou-te-esperando-father-i-am-waiting-you-2007-2008).

Judy Blankenship, who lives in Cañar, Ecuador, for half of each year, has become the area's community documentarian. She photographs residents and ritual events, records oral histories, and is creating a digital archive of her work and that of others—all done in collaboration with the people of Cañar. The digital Cultural Archive of Cañar will eventually be on the Internet. Blankenship began her work in the 1990s as a volunteer on a local research project, training two young indigenous men in photography and oral history. She continued the project with a Fulbright grant in 2000. Over two decades, Blankenship has deepened her friendships and kinship ties through teaching and ongoing photography. She shares her work with the community and created a scholarship fund for Cañari women to attend university.

To update friends in her other home of Portland, Oregon, Blankenship began sending e-mail accounts and photos of daily life in Cañar chronicles, which transformed into a blog titled *Cañar Chronicles: Life in the Andes of Ecuador* (http://judyblankenship.com/). Those missives also evolved into her first book, *Cañar: A Year in the Highlands of Ecuador* (2005). Eight years later, she and her husband Michael built a traditional style house, an experience recounted in *Our House in the Clouds: Creating a Second Life in the Andes of Ecuador* (2013). Blankenship's work exemplifies how careful observation and journals can blossom into books as well as blogs. But she also models documentation as witness. Collaboration and commitment to a community can create lasting impact.

Sometimes documentary work highlights broader global concerns. Guha Shankar, a folklife and multimedia documentary specialist at the American Folklife Center, Library of Congress, works with other national and international agencies to fuse cultural preservation and social justice. Shankar worked on one such project with colleagues from Duke University's Center for Documentary Studies, the Maasai Cultural Heritage Foundation in Kenya, and the World Intellectual Property Organization in Geneva. Part of the World Intellectual Property Organization's mission is to help indigenous groups protect intellectual property, including the right to authorize reproduction and use of images, oral tradition, music, crafts, and other aspects of heritage. To learn documentation skills, members of the Maasai community attended intensive fieldwork training at the Library of Congress, followed by hands-on documentary instruction at the Center for Documentary Studies in 2008. A year later, Shankar traveled with Tom Rankin, noted photographer and then-director of the Center for Documentary Studies, to Kenya to reinforce the original training. The project laptop, audio recorder, and camera remained with the Maasai. Beyond preserving cultural traditions, the community plans to record stories of historical conflicts and contemporary challenges.[23] These include the encroachment on their traditional grazing lands, language loss, and environmental catastrophes. As with Blankenship's project in Cañar, digital copies of the Maasai documentation live in multiple places, including the Library of Congress. Sharing resources creates access to these stories for a much wider audience.

REVISION

The variety of documentary forms can enliven the written word. But adding images or sound to writing often requires revision. If you physically describe a person you've interviewed, then later add a photo, you'll need to rewrite so you don't duplicate what's now visually obvious. But such practical matters aside, adding media can lend dimension, complexity, and depth to your presentation of experiences abroad.

Revision Exercise One

Search your memory for a scene that you photographed. Without looking at it again, write about what you remember of the photo, where and when you took it, what it means to you now. You might start with "from this distance [in time or space] . . ." Explore how your perception has changed. If you wrote about that image earlier, compare your original freewrite with the newer writing based on your remembrance.

Revision Exercise Two

Go back to the sounds you recorded in writing exercise 2 in this chapter. Find a new site to record, one very different from the original. Juxtapose the two recordings to create an audio postcard. You might contrast a marketplace or busy city square with a wetlands noisy with frogs, birds, and other wildlife.

Experiment with Form—Combine Word, Image, and Sound

Comb your notebook for freewrites that capture your most meaningful encounters. Choose one and read it aloud to find the heart of the story. Expand if you need to and then revise to create a narrative to run about five minutes when read aloud. Record your voice, adding music using GarageBand on your Mac or one of the alternatives for Windows PC. Now select images—photos from your journey, scanned pages from books, and other sources. Create a storyboard, laying out the sequence of sound, image, and text. Many websites give step-by-step instructions on how to create storyboards. The University of Houston's Educational Uses of Digital Storytelling is one such useful site (http://digitalstorytelling.coe.uh.edu/page.cfm?id=23&cid=23 &sublinkid=37).

Given the array of ways to record your travels, you might sometimes wish for James Agee's more limited world of documentary choices. You will probably use, as so many travelers have, multiple forms—scribbled notes, video clips, photographs, scanned museum copy, street sounds caught on the fly, interviews on your smart phone in a moment of crisis or a carefully planned oral history. In the end, what you make of each will depend on the reach of your imagination and your level of commitment. Perhaps, like Agee, you will still feel thwarted in trying to convey the transformative quality of cross-cultural experience. But our hunger for stories drives the work. As Robert Coles reminds us: "The call to documentary work is an aspect of the call of stories, of our wish to learn about one another through observation." These stories and pictures, he continues, are "a chance for us to wonder how we are doing as we try to affirm ourselves by reaching toward others, helping to make a difference in a neighborhood, a nation."[24]

5

—

PORTRAITS AND PROFILES

Your journal will likely fill with stories of people—encounters with strangers, strangers who become friends, friends who transform to mentors and offer an insider's view of a culture. Maybe you focused on the bent man on the bridge who greeted you each morning, the patient tutor who helped you master Chinese, or the family that embraced you as a guest.

The individual or group portrait is one of the most potent tools of the writer abroad. But how do we write about people? "The lives of other people are unknowable," says poet and memoirist Mark Doty—a discouraging thought when compounded by cultural difference.[1] Yet biographers face this challenge, as do travelers and ethnographers. Nonfiction writers fashion characters from observations of real people—how they look, how they act in daily life, what they own or use, and what they say. We can't capture an entire life through a month-long or even multiyear acquaintance.

Your vision of another person will be partial, just as your first-person narrator is not the living, breathing "you." But in telling your version of other people's stories, you can reach for deeper understanding of their lives. Details and dialogue provide material for creating vivid portraits.

THE SKETCH: PHYSICAL DESCRIPTION

Often, full portraits start as sketches. When Joanne met Mexican healer and artist Eva Castellanoz, she jotted a few lines in her journal: "Wide cheekbones, black permed hair edged by gray, wearing a white Mexican cotton blouse embroidered with blue and pink flowers." As with line drawings, sketches rely on minimal details. You're not creating a biography, at least not yet. Joanne went on to write *Remedios: The Healing Life of Eva Castellanoz*, but at this first meeting, she had no inkling of the friendship that would develop. Two decades later, the outline of that sketch grew. Since Eva had lived in the United States for many years, her clothing had always seemed just a reflection of ethnic pride. Then, during a visit to Portland from eastern Oregon, Eva told Joanne a story. She'd recently returned from a trip to Texas. At the airport, clerks initially ignored her, then sent her scurrying to the wrong gate. She nearly missed her flight. When she recounted this travail to a friend, the woman eyed Eva's embroidered blouse. "If you dressed differently, people would treat you better," the woman advised. "She meant 'look less Mexican,'" Eva said. Then she delivered a testimonial: "This is how I dress. This is who I am. I am the woman who scrubs your toilet. I am the woman who picks your corn. I am the woman who stands in the factory line. I'm here and I look this way. And I, too, am the image of God." Years later, while teaching in Mexico, Joanne gave a public talk and read this section from *Remedios*. In the audience, an older woman wept. Perhaps she saw a daughter who had emigrated north; perhaps she saw herself. Joanne knew only that her journal entry on an embroidered blouse, noted when she met Eva more than twenty years before, had finally found its way home.

So record your first impressions: the gold tooth, the cigar in the mouth, the stars glistening on a purple sari. Remember the craft discussion of descriptive detail in chapter 2. Try to create a mental picture for the reader. You don't know where it might lead.

Sometimes, friends and mentors surface in unlikely places. The *New Yorker* writer Peter Hessler offers the arresting example of Sayyid Ahmed, his garbage collector (*zabal*) in Cairo. "Tales of the Trash" is a classic literary profile, a form we discuss in the craft section of this chapter. Hessler opens with a description of the three doors in his Cairo apartment, one strictly for the use of Sayyid. After months of waking to a mysteriously clean balcony, the garbage whisked away before dawn, Hessler finally meets Sayyid. "He's not much taller than five feet, but his shoulders are broad and his legs are bowed from hauling weight. Usually, his clothes are several sizes too large, and his shoes flap like those of a clown, because he harvests them from the garbage of bigger men."[2] As we'll see, these details about Sayyid's work clothes become important later in the story.

Sometimes physical descriptions structure a piece of writing. Natalie Kusz shaped "Inscribed on the Body," a portrait of her father, around his scars. She begins, "Perceive him first, then, as his physical body," then recalls his nose, once broken while boxing; his skin and how she watched him shave when she was a child; the frostbite earned during Alaska's punishing winters.[3] Such details are signposts on the map of an essay, akin to the blue arrows that guide us along a trail in the woods.

Writing Exercise One

Make a list of the people you meet during your first week of traveling. Choose one and write a sketch based on details about his or her body, gestures, and facial expressions. Look for idiosyncratic features: she constantly runs her fingers through her hair; always urges you to eat more; leans to one side while walking.

NAMING NAMES

Names root us in particulars: not just a tree but a cottonwood. Not just any street but Avenue of the Revolution. Names uncover personal stories in social and historical context. In Mexico and some other parts of Latin America, names include a maternal and paternal surname, a practice that traces back to Spain. Anthropologist Clifford Geertz describes how names in Bali reflect ideas about "personhood." The Balinese have six types of labels—personal names; birth-order names; kinship terms; teknonyms (terms of relationship); status titles; and public titles. Of these, the little-used "personal" names are "treated as though they were military secrets."[4] In a culture where public life matters more than private affairs, a man or woman might go to the grave as the only one who remembers this name.

Names also connect us to place and to history. In *Number Our Days*, Barbara Myerhoff's ethnographic account of a community center for elderly Jews in Venice Beach, California, names root us in "Yiddishkeit" culture. Myerhoff bears witness to the gradual disappearance of an Eastern European Jewish diaspora that numbered near ten thousand in 1970s California. The center's residents have names like Basha, Shmuel, and Moshe; many belong to the Emma Lazarus Club, evoking the celebrated Jewish immigrant poet who wrote the famous lines about "your huddled masses yearning to breathe free" for the Statue of Liberty. Specific names create a foundation for the history and culture Myerhoff chronicles.

In some cultures, naming is storied and even poetic. Howard Norman collected and translated naming stories among the Swampy Cree in Canada. "Born Tying Knots" is one example. It begins: "When he came out, into the world, / the umbilical cord / was around his toes. / This didn't trouble us, / that he was tying knots *that* early. / We untied it." Norman reinforces an essential connection: "To say the name is to begin the story."[5]

Fieldwork Exercise One

Return to the list of people you've met. Do short interviews with two or three people about the origins of their names and how they feel about them. Follow up with library and/or Internet research about naming practices in their culture.

A caveat: you may chronicle the stories of people who don't want their names, location, or any other identifying information disclosed. In fraught political settings, such information may endanger someone's health or life. Some people simply want to guard their privacy. Conversely, individuals may welcome the acknowledgment. When possible, ask those who are generous enough to share their stories about their preference. Use pseudonyms when necessary.

THE MATERIAL WORLD: OBJECTS, CHARACTERS, AND DESIRE

In every culture, objects surround people. Things prompt stories, and stories uncover cultural meaning. In "Stuff," David Long writes, "In real life, we have complex psychological relationships to things . . . our histories are, in fact, histories of our tenancy in the universe of stuff."[6]

Even the poorest people have possessions that reveal cultural values. In *Walking the Gobi*, writer and adventurer Helen Thayer describes the meager physical world of a family that hosted her on the Mongolian Steppes: "The *ger* [a cone-shaped traditional house] lacked the usual embroidery and brightly colored dressers. A white ceramic Buddha sat on a plain box at the back of the *ger*, but there were no wall coverings and no carpet to cover the packed-dirt floor. The older woman, now a grandmother, immediately served us salty tea from a pan already heating on the stove."[7] Her description of the family's generosity wraps around the figure of the white Buddha overseeing life in a brutal landscape.

Peter Hessler's portrait of Sayyid Ahmed circles his subject's vast gleanings from garbage collecting. Around those objects, the illiterate Sayyid created a network of informal advisers to interpret unknown specimens like birth control pills (possible aphrodisiacs), Chinese medicine (maybe sex-related), half-empty bottles (which, if alcoholic, would have resale possibilities). Hessler eventually joins Sayyid on his garbage rounds as a participant observer. Along the way, Sayyid profiles the neighborhood: the man whose discarded syringes expose his diabetes, the foreign woman who has irked the landlord, the priest who's too cheap to tip. Here, the initial sketch based on Sayyid's clothing accrues meaning: "This is one of the reasons Sayyid dresses so poorly—he knows that dirty, ill-fitting clothes are more likely to inspire generosity."[8] Through these objects and related stories, we glimpse the workings of an informal but surprisingly effective system of trash collecting in an otherwise chaotic city.

Objects trigger memory through sensory details: the warp and weft of fabric, the feel of smooth stones in a garden, the smell of fresh tortillas on a *comal*. Careful journal notes lay the foundation for portraits.

Writing Exercise Two

Choose another person from your list or build on your initial sketch. Make a list of objects you associate with that person. Do a portrait shaped around a single object or write a short paragraph about each object and its place in that person's life.

STATUS DETAILS

Tom Wolfe, one of the originators of the New Journalism, created the term "status details" for the particulars of a person in social context: "everyday gestures, habits, manners, customs, styles of furniture, clothing, decoration, styles of traveling, eating, keeping house ... and other symbolic details that might exist within a scene."[9] These details may uncover social status but point to other characteristics as well.

Characters, says writer and teacher Janet Burroway, are defined by their desires. We share certain needs: food, shelter, and other basics. Additionally, some people want fortune and fame; others crave solitude and anonymity. We are idiosyncratic creatures also shaped by our culture. Material objects accrue varied meanings in different contexts. Denim jeans signaled status in the former Soviet Union in part because they symbolized freedom. But what do they mean in Mumbai today? In rural Papua New Guinea?

Status details often build on incongruities, confounding our expectations. When Sayyid invites Hessler to his home for a traditional birth ceremony, the author is surprised by the spanking newness of the apartment, the two televisions, the plastic-covered couches, a computer for Sayyid's son—objects that overturn Hessler's assumptions of a house furnished with garbage pickings. Sayyid's apartment also contrasts with his disheveled clothing. Further, Sayyid's wife turns out to be a beautiful, educated woman.

Hessler deftly integrates Sayyid's material life into the broader context of Egyptian religious and migration patterns. The garbage collection system, we learn, dates to the early 1900s when migrants from Egypt's Western Desert moved to Cairo and paid for the right to collect garbage and charge accordingly. Coptic Christians added to the mix in the 1930s and 1940s, raising pigs to eat organic garbage. Muslim middlemen managed the system.

Physical objects in the public realm tell larger cultural stories about economic and political relationships. Cars on Havana's streets are one example. American 1950s Chevys and Cadillacs represent Cuba's isolation following the 1960 U.S. trade embargo. Russian

Ladas arrived in 1970s and 1980s. Chinese-manufactured Geelys and South Korean Kias followed after the Cuban government's 2014 relaxation of limits on car purchases. Who owns which cars? What combination of money and influence bought that vehicle?

———————————— ————————————

Fieldwork Exercise Two

Make a list of objects frequently found in a culture. Start with things that are visible in public spaces, such as cars or clothing. Add a list of public services and resources you have questions about, such as water or control of telecommunications. Why are old Volkswagens the dominant cars? Who governs access to water or electricity or the Internet? Follow up with an interview and library research.

ROUND AND FLAT CHARACTERS

E. M. Forster first contrasted "round" characters—multidimensional and capable of change—with "flat" characters—static figures distinguished by a single characteristic. Though Forster described characters in fiction, his division serves nonfiction as well. Round characters are complex enough to surprise us. *Mountains beyond Mountains*, Tracy Kidder's compelling story of medical reformer Dr. Paul Farmer, is exemplary. Farmer emerges as quirky, sometimes monomaniacal, but fiercely devoted to the people he serves as a doctor and medical pioneer in Haiti and other parts of the world. We expect a full biography to chart such character development. However, you can strive for complex portraits of individuals you encounter abroad, even on brief acquaintance.

Peter Hessler's Sayyid is a round character. Despite his subject's self-deprecating description as "stupid, and fit only for the work of a donkey," he emerges as canny and socially perceptive.[10] But just as our sympathy deepens for an illiterate but street-savvy *zabal*, Hessler's story turns. We learn about Sayyid's unequal marriage, circumcision of his daughters, and other ways in which he embodies the attitudes of his class and culture—sensibilities Hessler finds sexist. Why, he asks, are men taking Viagra-like sex drugs while women are cloaked, circumcised, and homebound? When he details Sayyid's marital tensions, Hessler writes: "All the skill that Sayyid showed in Zamalek [Hessler's district in Cairo]—his insight and flexibility, his ability to interact and negotiate with so many different people—seemed to evaporate when he was dealing with his wife."[11]

We may want to alternately applaud and chastise Sayyid. We experience this round character through watching him talking, arguing, and interacting with family and customers. Seeing a character in action can highlight contradictions in personality. Though Hessler makes clear his opposition to sexism, he helps us see the *zabal* as a complex person acting in the world. But striving for cultural understanding doesn't mean excusing behavior you would consider a violation of rights in any context.

Writing Exercise Three

Return to your sketch or choose a new person from your list. Add scenes of the person in action: bartending, plowing a field, playing music. If possible, repeat more than once. Look for differences and possible contradictions in a person's actions. If a store clerk is normally friendly, what changed the morning he or she snapped at a customer? Look for incongruities to create round characters.

WHAT PEOPLE SAY: HEARING VOICES

As you make notes for a sketch, build toward a critical aspect of a portrait: integrating the person's voice. In chapter 3, we suggested fieldwork on the street to notice how people speak as well as what they say. Tone, choice of words, syntax, and "register"—the particular use of language in different settings—are all critical. In the last chapter, we discussed how to record and transcribe interviews. Later in this chapter, we delineate ways to write from transcripts. But if you're working from notes or memory, there are other ways to help a reader hear the voices that echo in our minds.

Consider how Kathleen Tyau invites the reader to hear a voice that shaped her youth. In "How to Cook Rice," she uses the second person to mimic her mother's instructions. We hear her mother speaking to her but the "you" also addresses us, the readers. "Cook rice the way I show you and it will always turn out right. . . . Did you wash your hands? And pin back your hair so it doesn't get in your eyes." Tyau folds her mother's dictums about proper behavior into the mundane details of cooking. "Don't sit in a boy's lap. And don't let him touch your personal."[12] "Your personal" captures an entire world that Tyau would have lost in a simple summary of her mother's attitudes toward sex.

The use of second person can pose problems; it calls attention to itself as a device. But the "you" voice also invites readers in, establishing a sense of immediacy.

----------------------------✔----------------------------

Writing Exercise Four

Write in the voice of one of your overseas teachers or someone you met while traveling. For example, choose your language teacher, hear his or her voice in your head and begin, "Say after me. . . ." Or recall a person who gave you directions: "Go west at the light . . ."

ETHICAL ISSUES

With luck and persistence, you'll record a range of different people while traveling. As you do so, explain your goals and the uses of the interview. For *Number Our Days*, anthropologist Barbara Myerhoff was intent on interviewing Shmuel, a resident of the Jewish community center in California where she conducted fieldwork. When she described her intentions, he initially refused. "So you want me to be your 'native.' No, that's flattering but not good. I'm not typical. . . . Find someone else."[13] Eventually, Shmuel yielded to Myerhoff's argument that she was not after "the typical" but sought his unique perspective. Thus began a very fruitful relationship.

Whether you're embarked on a project like Myerhoff's or living overseas like Peter Hessler, ethical issues saturate writing about people. Secrets may surface; trauma informs stories of economic hardship, war, or exile. Sexual assault and other forms of violence require extra vigilance. How do you decide whether and when to tell such stories?

Some people simply won't talk to you. Reasons for mistrust are many. They might be confused about your goals or where interviews will be housed. The ubiquitous nature of surveillance has made some people reluctant to grant interviews. Be sure to present yourself and your intentions honestly. Use pseudonyms if the person prefers anonymity. Try to give something back. You might offer digital copies of interviews, along with typed transcriptions. Some travelers do volunteer work as gift exchange. Cash payment is tricky. Journalists' professional ethics discourage such "checkbook journalism." The stance of professional ethnographers varies. Some, especially when grant-funded, offer honoraria to thank people for their time. But this is understood as a gesture, not a strict tit for tat exchange of money for information or stories.

Your response to these thorny questions may shift with your situation. Personal, religious, academic, or professional ethics offer guidelines. A journalist's article that could change government policy differs from a student's dilemma of whether to recount a host family's tragedy. Ethnographers owe allegiance to their subjects; they often share their writing with a cultural insider to check facts or nuances of meaning. Most journalists are accountable to a publisher as well as the broader public, and they tend to frown on showing writing to a source. Journalist Walt Harrington's story about a suicide is unusual in this regard. Harrington once broke the *Washington Post*'s rule never to show a subject a story before publication. Because of his topic, he felt ethically bound to read the entire story aloud to the family in advance. If his editor had challenged him, his "flimsy excuse" was that he hadn't actually *shown* them the story. The family didn't ask for any changes, and Harrington felt sure he'd done the right thing. He argues that journalists must "claim the right to determine their own ethical relationships."[14] Deciding which stories to tell and when and where to publish them will depend on circumstances. But Harrington's thoughts about ethics offer a useful model.

CRAFT DISCUSSION: WRITING FROM INTERVIEWS

Edited Oral Histories

With transcript in hand, how do you write the story? One tried and true method is the edited oral history. Writer and radio host Studs Terkel mastered this style in his numerous books, from *Working: People Talk about What They Do All Day and How They Feel About What They Do* (1974) to his last publication *P.S.: Further Thoughts from a Lifetime of Listening* (2008). Terkel dug for the marrow of each interview. He linked individual accounts to social movements, highlighting shared themes and human dilemmas. He often opened with a short bio or a description of the interview setting. Consider the following story of artist Jacob Lawrence in Terkel's *Coming of Age: The Story of Our Century by Those Who've Lived It*:

SEATTLE, WASHINGTON

We're in his studio on the second floor of his frame house, where he lives with his wife, Gwen, also a painter. On the walls are some of his works in progress. On the tables are hand tools: hammer, chisel, plane, brushes. There is an impromptu, easy touch here; not at all precisely arranged. Everything he may need appears to be comfortably at hand.

He retired from teaching at the University of Washington nine years ago.

This is what my day is like. I sit here, I'm looking at my works, I'm reading, I'll go back to my drawing table, do some drawing. That's more or less it. Of course we go shopping because we have to eat. But this is my place, this is where I work.

I work constantly. I look at my tools here. I'm not a cabinetmaker, but I use them. I love to look at hand tools. They're beautiful to see, to feel. They're a symbol of working, of building. I use them that way. . . . I use them in my paintings as I would in a still life. To me, these tools are alive.[15]

Terkel focused on Lawrence's art, culling the core of the interview to render essential elements of his life and work in a few pages.

Belarusian writer Svetlana Alexievich skillfully edited interviews to evoke the atrocity of the 1986 Chernobyl nuclear explosion. The stories encapsulate the enormity of the disaster through intimate details of victims' lives. Here is the voice of Lyudmilla Ignatenko, the wife of deceased fireman Vasily Ignatenko. She was pregnant at the time of the explosion: "We were newlyweds. We still walked around holding hands, even if we were just going to the store. I would say to him, 'I love you.' But I didn't know then how much. I had no idea. . . ." Lyudmilla recounts finding her husband in the hospital and the shock of his gradual disintegration: "There's a fragment of some conversation, I'm remembering it. Someone saying: 'You have to understand: This is not your husband anymore, not a beloved person, but a radioactive object with a strong density of poisoning. You're not suicidal. Get a hold of yourself.' And I was like someone who'd lost her mind: 'But I love him! I love him!' He's sleeping, and I'm whispering: 'I love you!' Walking in the hospital courtyard, 'I love you.' Carrying his sanitary tray, 'I love you.'" After Lyudmilla's baby is born: "They showed her to me—a girl. 'Natashenka,' I called out. 'Your father named you Natashenka.' She looked healthy. Arms, legs. But she had cirrhosis of the liver. Her liver had twenty-eight roentgens. Congenital heart disease. Four hours later they told me she was dead." Alexievich grounds Lyudmilla's story in the collective experience of the sufferers and by extension, in universal fears:

There are many of us here. A whole street. That's what it's called—Chernobylskaya. . . . No one's asked what we've been through. What we saw. No one wants to hear about death. About what scares them.

But I was telling you about love. About my love . . .[16]

The Profile

The terms "portrait" and "profile" are sometimes used interchangeably. "Portrait" suggests a painting's vivid details. The literary profile has a distinct history. The *New Yorker* editor David Remnick describes it as "a concise rendering of a life through anecdote, incident, interview, and description."[17] Many credit the magazine's founding editor, Harold Ross, with invention of the profile. Remnick wryly notes the hubris of placing Ross "ahead of Plutarch, Defoe, Aubrey, Strachey," and others. The profile clearly has deep historical roots, but contemporary writers have altered its features.

Profiles build on extensive interviews and observations. While oral historians shape a story around first-person accounts, profile writers use the third person mixed with the subject's voice. In many profiles, the writer is invisible. In others, the authorial "I" appears as the writer weaves in and out of the story. Profiles range widely in style and form. Remnick notes, "The thing about the profile—with the exception of the parameter that it has to be true, where its facts have to be facts, and I'm a big believer in that, in a conservative sense—everything else can be radical. Structure, sentence structure, word choice, descriptive powers . . . all those tools that are open to you as a literary writer should be open to you as a profile writer."[18]

Some profiles start with setting. Calvin Tomkin's story of high-wire walker Philippe Petit begins: "From the departure point, the void hits you like a thunderclap. It is sixteen hundred feet down,

104   ENCOUNTERING CULTURES

straight down, to the meandering bed of the Little Colorado River. The distance across, to the isolated mesa on the other side, which Philippe Petit will walk to on his cable, is twelve hundred feet."[19] You fear for Petit from the first page, imagining his possible demise.

Physical descriptions can draw readers into a story. Here is the opening of Philip Garrison's profile of Arturo, a Mexican migrant worker in Washington state who has landed in prison: "It was episodes of Kojak that had given Arturo his first (dubbed) glimpse of the country he sat in now, wearing orange overalls, talking through plate glass, running his fingers through thick hair that his wife scissored monthly on the front stoop. Fingers thick with flat nails and knuckles big as walnuts. The feed-sack build of him emitted a voice as thin as flute notes."[20]

Like other forms of nonfiction, profiles combine summaries and backstory with scenes. Dialogue in scenes should move the story forward, add emotion or interest, or reveal aspects of character. Exemplary is Hessler's mix of description and dialogue between Sayyid and a lawyer when the *zabal* seeks a possible divorce. The lawyer appears, "a short, neckless man who leaned forward as he talked, shoulders level with his ears, as if prepared to ram his head into whatever stood in his way." He urges Sayyid to be tough, holding up the court documents his wife filed. "'Look at this!' 'I can't read,' Sayyid said. 'She insults you with nasty words! She writes these things—look at it!'" the lawyer counters. "'I can't read,' Sayyid said."[21] The *zabal*'s illiteracy makes him suddenly vulnerable—an emotional effect achieved through dialogue. Despite Sayyid's sexism toward his wife, the reader's stance might soften.

You can use direct quotes from interviews or re-create dialogue from memory, depending on your purpose and genre. Hessler, as a journalist, likely relied on careful notes or recordings. Even with an audio record, thoughtful editing is essential to avoid misrepresenting someone's speech. With memoir and other forms of literary nonfiction, re-creating dialogue is now accepted. But this can be murky terrain, especially when writing about events long past.

So hew to the truth as you remember it. When in doubt, give the reader a signal. Use phrases such as "I think it was like this . . ." or "the conductor may have said . . ." or "I imagine that . . ."

When working from notes in a language you don't know well, consult a native speaker. The speech should sound believable to someone from that culture.

Some profiles circle descriptions of a person by others—friends, family members, coworkers. In *Moonshine: A Life in Pursuit of White Liquor*, Alec Wilkinson builds an entire chapter on quirky, sometimes contradictory quotes from people who knew Garland Bunting. A "still detective" hell-bent on prosecuting North Carolina's moonshine producers, Bunting has spent plenty of time in court. One chapter lists what lawyers have said about him:

"Garland does an excellent job in court. He's well prepared and very believable."
"Garland testifies straight down the line, always. Nothing but the absolute truth."
"Garland's always one step ahead, and it makes it pretty difficult to fight him."
"I'd rather sit back and listen to Garland talk than go to the bank."
"You can't put Garland in a position where he's scared."
"Garland can change from one kind of person to the other like you can snap your fingers."
"Garland's the type of person that will just kill you in court."[22]

Sometimes, a group of voices bests represents a topic of shared importance. Svetlana Alexievich interviewed numerous people about the Chernobyl disaster. Her portraits are collective as well as individual. Here are segments from the section titled "Settlers' Chorus: Those Who Returned":

Oh, I don't even want to remember it. It was scary. They chased us out, the soldiers chased us. The big military machines rolled in. The all-terrain ones. One old man—he was already on the ground. Dying. Where was he going to go? "I'll just get up," he was crying, "and walk to the cemetery. I'll do it myself."

We were leaving—I took some earth from my mother's grave, put it in a little sack. Got down on my knees: "Forgive us for leaving you." I went there at night and I wasn't scared. People were writing their names on the houses. On the wood. On the fences. On the asphalt.

Alexievich creates a counterpoint with "Soldiers' Chorus." The kaleidoscope of views intensifies the stories' emotional power. "Our regiment was given the alarm. It was only when we got to the Belorusskaya train station in Moscow that they told us where we were going. One guy, I think he was from Leningrad, began to protest. They told him they'd drag him before a military tribunal. The commander said exactly that before the troops: 'You'll go to jail or be shot.' I had other feelings, the complete opposite of that guy. I wanted to do something heroic."[23]

Writing Exercise Five—Two Models

Do a freewrite based on what you learned from an interview. Then survey the interview transcript carefully. Underline phrases or highlight segments that seem important. List recurrent themes that might structure the piece. Do a keyword search. If someone talks repeatedly about how migration shaped his or her life, this may be the heart of the story.

1. Edited Life History. Write a brief biography and/or contextual description as an introduction, then, following Terkel and Alexievich, use the narrator's words to tell the story. Choose segments from the transcript that illuminate the chosen theme.

2. The Profile. Start with a description of the person, the setting, or some central scene from his or her story. Select quotes from the interview and write a third-person profile building on one selected topic. Refrain from using first person or describing your presence.

REVISION

Portraits and profiles can encourage empathy by bringing us into the lives of others. Consider the emotional power of Svetlana Alexievich's oral history or Hessler's surprising revelations about the life of an Egyptian garbage collector. When we turn from observer to witness, we discover the fullness of people often invisible or poorly understood. Well-developed, vivid portraits can overturn stereotypes. Revising your oral histories and profiles now can add depth, confront possible misconceptions, and explore new formal possibilities.

Revision Exercise One

Return to the life history interview you edited (part 1 of writing exercise 5 above). Underline key quotes and write in response to them. Why do they seem important? What was the person trying to tell you? Then, use each keyword or quote as the basis for a lyric essay, writing a short piece about each one.

Revision Exercise Two

Reread the profile you wrote (part 2 of writing exercise 5 above). If you began with a description of the person, start a revised version with the setting. Since you wrote strictly in third person, you can now add scenes in which you are present, observing and participating.

Experiment with Form—a Group Portrait

One way to document a group is through juxtaposing voices, as in Alexievich's "Settlers' Chorus." Pick a central theme from your interview or find a new subject to explore. Do interviews with at least two other people to find shared and divergent points of view. Then, following Alexievich, create an ensemble of voices surrounding the theme. You can juxtapose the subjects' words to show different perspectives or create a third-person portrait that integrates quotes.

Japanese novelist Haruki Murakami said of his work, "I think that my job is to observe people and the world, and not to judge them. I always hope to position myself away from so-called conclusions. I would like to leave everything wide open to all the possibilities in the world."[24] In writing about people, we need to stay open to surprise and to share that wonder with the reader.

Peter Hessler ends his story about Sayyid Ahmed with a description of the political scene. After President Morsi's ejection from politics in 2013, Egyptians returned to where they started, seeking comfort in the familiar. Despite ongoing conflict, Sayyid and many others settled back into family life; the country as a whole fell into a familiar pattern of frustration. The devil you know. "Still, they survived," writes Hessler. "The circle kept turning. The garbage vanished from the fire escape every morning." Sayyid resumed taking drugs to enhance his sex life, which Hessler concludes, "had to mean something."[25] What that something is remains open to the reader's interpretation.

6

—

WRITING ABOUT PLACE

The novelist, travel writer, and teacher Bob Shacochis tells students that good fiction or nonfiction should make *setting* as much a living entity as human character.[1] Physical environment shapes us all, and creating a sense of place is crucial in telling stories. To be in an affecting place is like meeting a remarkable person, triggering anxiety and confusion, or curiosity and excitement. The temperament of a place emerges in things you see, smell, touch, and hear. All the sensual details that came into play in previous chapters are important here.

As we travel, we are sojourners and observers but also "field-workers" plowing the ground for meaning. But "the field," as anthropologist and writer Kirin Narayan argues, might be a bounded setting—a city like Baltimore or a favela in Rio de Janeiro—or more diffuse—high-tech firms spread out over five countries. Each will offer a different sense of place.[2] Think of an example close to home, like your neighborhood. Recall specifics, such as a building's architecture or the way the streets wind through town or the effects of the weather. Remember Cynthia Ozick's contrast of a visitor who "passes through a place" with the pilgrim whom the "place passes through."[3] Readers want to absorb the experience of a place.

Travel writing hasn't always evoked setting in such impressionistic ways. The genre has evolved, as Peter Whitfield argues, from mere reporting into a form of writing that re-creates how it felt to be there, far from home. Through time, Whitfield says, "travel writing acquired depth and honesty, humility and vision."[4] He cites works such as Apsley Cherry-Garrard's *The Worst Journey in the World*, which captures part of the doomed 1912 Scott expedition to the Antarctic. Robert Falcon Scott and four other men died of starvation and exposure. But the field notes Scott left behind and the writing of people like Cherry-Garrard—a surviving member of the expedition—helped turn Scott into a British national hero. As Whitfield suggests, Scott's story of failure and death "forced people to re-examine what success and failure mean."[5] Later, American writers such as Barry Lopez and Gretel Ehrlich pushed travel writing into moral investigations of environmental issues. Other writers have incorporated food, music, and other themes into travel stories.

For Peter, an important element in writing about the ecological and visual character of West Africa, and Mali in particular, is the presence of iron in the soil. It sometimes turns the ground a deep maroon, like dried blood. Dirt roads cut startling red pathways through green forests or across plains of yellow grass. The ground along the Mali–Côte d'Ivoire border has the same red tinge. At times the color contrast between soil and foliage can disturb in a visceral way, raising images of blood coursing through veins. For a writer, this information is useful for adding visual depth to a narrative.

PLACE AS CHARACTER

Try to think of the place you're writing about as having a personality and attitude. What is it about this setting that separates it from any other? Consider how Luís Alberto Urrea personifies the Sonoran Desert along the U.S.-Mexico border in his book, *The Devil's Highway*:

The plants are noxious and spiked. Saguaros, nopales, the fiendish chol-las. Each long cholla spike has a small barb, and they hook into the skin, and they catch in elbow creases and hook forearm and biceps together. Even the green mesquite trees have long thorns set just at eye level. . . . The kissing bug bites you and its poison makes the entire body erupt in red welts. Fungus drifts on the valley dust, and it sinks into the lungs and throbs to live. The millennium has added a further danger: all wild bees in southern Arizona, naturalists report, are now Africanized. As if the desert felt it hadn't made its point, it added killer bees.[6]

How does Urrea give the place a "speaking role"? What details stay with you? Once you've established the character of a place, re-turn to those details as you write. Urrea weaves the desert's threats into his entire story, never letting us forget the terrors held there.

Writing Exercise One

In your new environment, try to identify the personality of a given place. Brainstorm a list of ten words you associate with this landscape (inte-riorscape, cityscape, townscape), positive and negative. These might be physical sites—sand dunes, florescent lights—or feelings and sensations—frightening, dank at dusk. Beginning with the first term, write a paragraph or tell a story about each aspect of the place. Read through your freewrites to find what connects each segment and then write on the thread you found. Pay attention to how that thread crosses from one section to the next.

CROSSING BORDERS

In Graham Greene's 1939 travel book about Mexico during the revolution, he writes, "The atmosphere of the border—it is like starting over again; there is something about it like a good confes-sion."[7] He goes on to describe crossing from El Paso, Texas, into

Ciudad Juarez. But before showing us the physical border, Greene, a convert to Catholicism, tries to capture something deeper and more startling about border crossings. His use of the metaphor of confession, a Catholic ritual sacrament, is important because Mexico banned the Catholic Church during the revolution of the early twentieth century. If we follow Greene's thinking, a border signals certain change, though the specifics are unknowable until the traveler passes into the new setting.

Open up the metaphor of the border and you find intriguing situations where stories live: a border crossing is a place or situation in flux, a political boundary or passage from the safety and warmth of your home and out into the world. Borders are geographic, spiritual, economic, ecological, linguistic, historical, social, political, and much more. Until you adjust, you are in that in-between zone.

Peter entered such a zone in 2011 during a border crossing from Mali, a country at peace, into Côte d'Ivoire, which was emerging from a decade-long civil war. In the front seat of a rented taxi, Peter was on his way to an interview. In the backseat was the driver's brother. After leaving Mali, they arrived at the Côte d'Ivoire checkpoint: a concrete blockhouse with the orange, white, and green Ivorian tricolor flying from a metal pole. A policeman, bent down with his hands on his knees, greeted Peter and his companions in Bambara. He declined to look at Peter's passport and turned to talk to the driver's brother. In French, the policeman asked for his identity papers. Glancing back, Peter saw he produced no papers at all: no passport, no identity card.

The policeman then spoke in Bambara to the driver, gestured at his brother, smiled and stepped back from the car. Later, Peter asked the driver why his brother had no papers. "He is my brother and I speak for him," the driver said, visibly annoyed. He squinted at Peter and wagged his finger. "You need to relax."

Here, Peter confronted "more than a customs house" as Greene described border crossings. He'd crossed not only the Mali–Côte d'Ivoire border of war and peace but also unstated cultural rules about legality and authority.

In countless works of fiction and nonfiction, the unstable place gives off a natural energy, the possibility of conflict and the unexpected. Extend the "nerve point" we identified in chapter 2 to that physical spot or situation that makes you uncomfortable or inspires fear. You might feel unstable walking along a cliff in darkness or sitting down to Thanksgiving dinner with your family or crossing borders between cultures, languages, or political or religious value systems.

The place where energy is volatile propels a story forward. It's also a good metaphor for place and travel as an act of transition. Each border presents a multilayered experience of moving from one state of mind to another. As Graham Greene says, once you've passed through a border, "Life is never going to be quite the same again," as if the act of crossing rearranges your molecules.[8]

Writing Exercise Two

Freewrite on your definition of a border. Then write about a significant border crossing you've made. Explore the environment, what it looked like, and how it made you feel in crossing. You might cast that experience in scene to sharpen the visual expression of action and setting.

CREATING AND USING MAPS

A map, in its raw form, attempts to harness a landscape within the framework of a piece of paper. John Noble Wilford opens his book, *The Mapmakers*, in 1972 at Dana Butte in the Grand Canyon, with its commanding panoramic view. Wilford was traveling with cartographers on a mapping mission. The party reached the butte's pinnacle, which "stood out in defiance of the winds and floods that had shaped it and everything around as far as the eye could see. . . . We could see and be seen from all directions." Wilford writes of being intimidated by the "primeval wonder" that is the Grand Canyon. "We came away knowing the ageless compulsion to reach out and, through mapping's ever-widening embrace of worlds, to reduce wonder to a scale more susceptible of human comprehension."[9]

But maps also reveal political and social perspectives. In *No Word for Welcome: The Mexican Village Faces the Global Economy*, Wendy Call describes the importance of maps in her writing about the impact of development in Mexico's Isthmus of Tehuantepec. The divergent maps she found exposed conflicts between indigenous people's lives and development planners' schemes.

On a shimmering Pacific coast beach an indigenous Huave fisherman traces through the sand with a stick. In a shaky hand he draws the path of his people's maritime migration to the isthmus one thousand years earlier. In the shade of a thatched hut another fisherman swings his arms through the late evening's sapphire air, tracing the migration of the shrimp he will catch later that night. On a coastal map stretched across a wide mahogany desk a government official shows a curious visitor potential sites for industrial shrimp farms. In front of a one-room adobe house an indigenous Mixe man holds up a full-color map of the isthmus and traces a line: where the government plans to slice a new highway through the village's farmland and forest.[10]

Wendy Call shows how each map—oral, sand-inscribed, different readings of colored marks on paper—reveals divergent worldviews. Travelers can't live without maps but must also be wary of what they see there. Take the case of the Mountains of Kong in West Africa. For centuries, European cartographers speculated that melting snow from high alpine mountains fed inland to West Africa's rivers and streams. Yet no one had visited these mountains. The Scottish explorer Mungo Park vaguely claimed to have seen them from near the banks of the Niger River in 1796. Based on Park's report, they appeared on maps until 1889 when a French naval officer crossed the entire region and declared the mountains a myth.

"What is intriguing about the Kong Mountains," wrote University of Illinois geographer Thomas J. Bassett, "is that they never existed except in the imaginations of explorers, mapmakers, and merchants."[11] Yet for two centuries they raised European hopes of snow-filled mountains that watered the West Africa's fertile plains. The mountains served as justification for exploration and colonization. Over the centuries, maps have shown the United States and Europe to be centers of the globe and larger than their actual sizes in relation to rival or poorer continents. But distortion is inevitable as the geographer and scholar Mark Monmonier explains in his book, *How to Lie with Maps*: "Not only is it easy to lie with maps, it's essential. To portray meaningful relationships with a complex, three-dimensional world on a flat sheet of paper or a video screen, a map must distort reality."[12]

When the writer George Packer received his Peace Corps assignment to Togo, in West Africa, just before graduating from college, he consulted a map at a library. "The country was still labeled with its colonial name, Togoland," he writes in his 1984 memoir, *Village of Waiting*, "a sliver squeezed into the West African coast among a crazy patchwork of borders."[13] That bit of research gave Packer and the reader an initial first impression of the country he would write about for another 314 pages. The map was confusing, but that "crazy patchwork of borders" accurately reflected the colonial history of Togo and West Africa. It was a start. Packer, now a well-known writer for the *New Yorker*, has been writing about international topics, including Francophone Africa, ever since.

Local maps uncover indigenous perspectives on a place. One self-taught cartographer—Aaron Carapella from Oklahoma—revised the geographic image of the United States with a series of new maps showing where Indian tribes existed before Europeans arrived. The maps at Carapella's website, Tribal Nations Maps, allow you to consider how they present the story of North America from a new perspective (http://tribalnationsmaps.com).

Fieldwork Exercise One

Do some fact-checking with maps. Find copies of maps in local shops, the library, and elsewhere. If you copied maps before you left home, compare with those you discover on-site. Describe what you see and what you think the mapmaker saw. Then, ask a resident to explain the landmarks on this map based on his or her own observations. What are the conflicts and/or correspondences between established maps and local people's stories?

You can also draw your own physical maps of places—a way to chart your evolving understanding of where you are and get feedback from residents. Maps reveal not just physical space—the grids of streets, the arrangement of desks in a classroom, seating at a formal dinner, the size and shape of garden plots—but the relationships between people and cultural beliefs. Your map will depend on your goals, whether you're in an urban or rural environment, and your access to private space.

Don't worry if you lack artistic skill. Drawing maps with visual details trains your eye and heightens your awareness. Always attend to the senses, recording smells, tastes, and visual details. You might make a sensory map—a scentscape, a soundscape, or a graphic story that captures images you encounter.

Mapping helps you pay attention to cultural rules for life in this new place and invites detailed descriptive writing. This close reading of place doesn't work if you are using a GPS unit, which makes the job too easy. You've got to walk the ground with your eyes and ears and, if necessary, your map open.

Fieldwork Exercise Two

Wherever you are, begin by mapping the streets, the churches, the restaurants, and sites of recreation and work. Is there a soccer yard? Places where only men or only women are allowed? Choose a village square, a market with food stalls, and add details. Include orientation (north, south, east, and west), buildings and other structures, traffic lights, an indication of the scale, and dates of the map. Then ask someone to travel that area with you, explaining what they see in their own community. Interviews on-site reveal much different information than those done in an office or home.

QUIRKS OF LANGUAGE AND EXPLOITED LANDSCAPES

As we saw in chapter 3 with street names, language connects to place. In Britain, a common word for bridge is "flyover." The word often leads to misunderstandings, even with English-speaking Americans. But the image makes sense—a pathway that "flies" over something. The edited collection *Homeground: Language for an American Landscape* captures the unique geographical and cultural features of place names in the United States. Often, stories rooted in places live only in oral tradition and may disappear. One contributor, Stephen Graham Jones, describes "Racetrack Valley," which "within Death Valley is called Racetrack Playa, a dry lakebed with a very fine clay surface. The term racetrack comes from the trails or tracks the lakebed's rocks leave behind them when they 'race'—that is, mysteriously slide along the floor of the lakebed."[14]

Asking for directions can uncover a certain regional logic as well as cultural rules for behavior. In Northern Ireland, where people are unfailingly polite and helpful, Joanne found that strangers would give her detailed directions to a place even when they didn't know where it was. To say "I don't know" seemed inhospitable. Giving directions often became an occasion for storytelling.

Increasingly, environmental issues raise ethical questions for travelers. How do you weigh where to visit and with whom? Ecotourism in many countries has helped develop local economies, provide jobs, and preserve the environment. On the other side, unchecked tourism can degrade the land or stymy development efforts local people may welcome. Tourism might exploit traditional ways of life. Making handmade tortillas, for example, may satisfy visitors' longing for authenticity while thwarting women's opportunities. The writer's first challenge is to comprehend how the land and environmental issues connect to people's lives. Experimentation with writing can then bring the reader into that experience with the complexities intact.

Leslie Jamison's essay "Pain Tours (I)" provides a compelling example. She begins her description of touring a Bolivian silver mine: "This is how you visit the silver mines of Potosí . . ." Jamison's intimate second-person voice carries us into the mine's wretched conditions, making us participants and observers. "Sometimes you have to kneel. Sometimes you have to crawl"; "you are having a little trouble breathing."[15] If, like Jamison, we feel the stab of privilege, we may feel guilty. We want action on the miners' behalf. There is no simple answer but the voice and structure of the essay urge the reader to witness.

Writing Exercise Three

Make a list of places you've visited, including some that troubled you. Then, following Jamison, use second person—the voice that offers instruction—to describe how to get there and what the reader will witness. Begin with "To get here, you must . . ." and follow with, "Then you begin to see . . ."

MYTHIC PLACES AND DARK HISTORIES

Here's another obstacle for writers: how to write about places that have been described so often they're now mythic. Paris, the Grand

Canyon, the Great Wall of China—the list is extensive. To get past romanticized images, writer David Sedaris eschewed the famous cafés of Paris in favor of mundane settings such as his dentist's office. In "Dentists without Borders," he describes the scene:

"I had braces when I was young, but maybe I need them again," I told her. An American dentist would have referred me to an orthodontist, but, to Dr. Barras, I was being hysterical. "You have what we in France call 'good-time teeth,'" she said. "Why on earth would you want to change them?" "Um, because I can floss with the sash to my bathrobe?" "Hey," she said. "Enough with the flossing. You have better ways to spend your evenings." I guess that's where the good times come in.[16]

The African American writer Eddy L. Harris found a fresh way write about the American South by immersing himself in its darkest history—slavery—and the civil rights struggles of the 1950s and 1960s. He opens *South of Haunted Dreams: A Ride through Slavery's Old Back Yard* by describing how he felt crossing this territory on his motorcycle. "I hold on tight . . . hurry past evil spirits. . . . These many years later, the South still owns my nightmares and haunts my memory."[17] Harris wants to find out how the South has evolved but he begins his journey in anger and fear as he struggles to tell a new story.

Harris's work reminds us that writing about a place with new vision requires novel language. Chekhov was firm on the need to reject overused language. In a letter to his brother in 1886, he wrote:

I think descriptions of nature should be very short and always be *à propos*. Commonplaces like "The setting sun, sinking into the waves of the darkening sea, cast its purple gold rays, etc.," "Swallows, flitting over the surface of the water, twittered gaily"—eliminate such commonplaces. You have to choose small details in describing nature, grouping them in such a way that if you close your eyes after reading it you can picture the whole thing. For example, you'll get a picture of a moonlit night if you write that on the dam of the mill a piece of broken bottle flashed like a bright star and the black shadow of a dog or a wolf rolled by like a ball.[18]

Writing Exercise Four

Try Sedaris's method of describing a pedestrian setting, using dialogue and scene. Then, following Chekhov, use indirection to show us a landscape, something akin to the rolling shadow of the dog or the wolf.

ENGAGEMENT WITH THE NATURAL WORLD

The writer Sara Wheeler spent seven months in Antarctica to write *Terra Incognita*. Her work encapsulates a sense of the South Pole and the people who live there. Against the backdrop of eternal winter, all normal sense of time fades. "The most significant thing from a writer's point of view," she told an interviewer, "is how [the place] affects you when you are totally loose, not just from your own cultural moorings but from any cultural moorings.... The Antarctic... is the ultimate tabula rasa ... nature in its most austere and most brutal."[19]

In similar fashion, the naturalist Craig Childs writes of his years poking around Anasazi ruins in the American Southwest. One day he and a friend disrobed, except for their boots, to ride a flashflood down a canyon to get close to an Anasazi great house. An extreme research method, perhaps, but Childs said what he discovered brought him closer to the terrain. "In my flesh," he wrote in *House of Rain: Tracking a Vanished Civilization across the American Southwest*, "I felt the weight of water, the flood absorbed into calluses and fingertips." Then, before walking among ruins, Childs took off his boots in order to sharpen his senses. "I let my bare feet feel the ground, aware of every pebble and stick.... Walls and parts of walls stood here and there.... Ceiling timbers as big as ship masts stuck out of the ground where rooms had buckled and caved in."[20]

Childs's descriptive style helps the reader both see and feel the enormity and vividness of landscape. Visual details, simile, and metaphor work to orient the reader toward the story's physical setting.

The writer Andrew X. Pham, who came to the United States from Vietnam as a boy, returned to his home country in the 1990s and crossed it by bicycle, which offered him a visceral connection to the place and its people. In *Catfish and Mandala: A Two-Wheeled Voyage through the Landscape and Memory of Vietnam*, he describes the rough ride in unrelenting heat. "I crunch through the morning, taking a ten-minute break every hour-and-a-half in the saddle. . . . Scattered every few miles on the side of the road are thatched lean-tos. . . . A boy, sometimes a man, curls up like a dog, out of the sun's fury, selling live crabs tied up in bunches like bananas. Occasionally, he dips the crabs into the water of the rice paddies to keep them alive."[21]

Writing Exercise Five

Make a list of places you've traveled and the physical details that define them, like the images and sounds of dense traffic in Beijing. Then, make a list of similes such as "Beijing is like an orchestra made entirely of drums and horns." Repeat this exercise with metaphors. Write a short paragraph using each simile or metaphor to describe the place.

EVOKING HISTORY THROUGH PLACE

The ideal traveler does research before embarking—checking out books, articles, websites, and maps. Anything you can find about the history and context of a place can revitalize the ghosts of the past.

The physical features of a forgotten landscape and the vocabulary of an era also locate a reader in time. To evoke the winter of 1939 in London, you could describe the smoke, the dankness and fear beneath dark and heavy rain clouds just before the outbreak of World War II. You could also weave in the "Keep Calm and Carry On" posters the government created to counter fear and boost morale before the predicted air strikes happened. Such details root us in a historical period through indirect but vivid means.

Walk through a camel market in remote northern Africa and you brush against the fourteenth century, when the camel caravan ruled trade from sub-Saharan Africa to the Mediterranean. Gold traveled north and east to Europe and the Middle East on these animals. When the caravans returned south with cloth and spices, Arab missionaries traveled with them, spreading Islam with poetry and sermon. The sight of these beasts, and men in ankle length djellaba robes and turbans, bartering in many languages, takes you out of your own time. Then, on the edge of the market, you see a row of heavy diesel-powered trucks, pulling flatbed trailers. They carry tons of grain in white sacks. On the trailer walls, the drivers have painted expressions of faith in English or French or Arabic: "Only God Knows" or "Dieu est mon co-pilot" or "Insh'Allah" (God willing). As your eyes bounce between camels and trucks, you see men transferring grain from the trucks to the backs of the camels. The beasts will carry the grain across lands too rugged for rubber tires.

Knowing history—political, ecological, spiritual, and more—is critical to understanding place. Every country was part of something else before the rise of the nation-state. Germany was part of the Holy Roman Empire, then a collection of small kingdoms at war with each other before they united in the nineteenth century, in part to defend against French invasion. Washington, DC's intensely humid summers remind you that it was built on a wetland that the Delaware Indians once fished and farmed. The Ottoman Empire once encompassed parts of South Europe, North Africa, and Asia. Fierce resentments linger among people whose newly divided countries became "the Balkans" after World War I.

In *Balkan Ghosts: A Journey through History*, Robert Kaplan weaves history into arresting scenes that build a sense of place. He also uncovers local versions of history. While traveling in Serbia in an area that is now Kosovo, he visits Mother Tatiana, an Orthodox Serbian nun, at the medieval Grachanitsa Monastery. Together they enter a building Kaplan recognizes as of Turkish design, with "madder

roof tiles, yellow stone walls, and overhanging wooden balconies."
Mother Tatiana, however, describes it as "typical Serbian architecture." In Bulgaria, the same design is "typical Bulgarian revivalist,"
while in Greece . . . you can guess the rest. Kaplan cites the monastery as one of two places that form part of Serbia's collective identity. The other is Kossovo Polje, the "Field of Black Birds," the site
of the 1389 defeat of the Serbs by the Turks, so-called because the
bodies were left for the carrion birds. The field provides one of Kaplan's startling juxtapositions concerning place and history: "While
1989 will be remembered by other peoples as the year when the
Cold War ended and the Communist system collapsed, for Mother
Tatiana and 8.55 million Serbs, 1989 signified something altogether
different: the six hundredth anniversary of their defeat."[22]

History can be hard to unearth, which heightens the thrill of
discovery. Robert Kaplan came to understand this by picking his
way across a land torn by ethnic strife and history unforgotten.
Tough journeys also make good stories. But some travel destinations deliver history through staged events. The changing of the
guard at London's Buckingham Palace is an example. Such spec-
tacles can be misleading, dependent on cliché and theater, like the
"Old West" gun fights that play out every summer day at noon
in Silverton, Colorado, a rough mining town in the 1800s that
now survives as a result of tourism. Staged events and packaged
experiences like Mount Rushmore are a culture unto themselves.
Tony Horowitz studied them for his book, *A Voyage Long and
Strange: Rediscovering the New World*. Starting at Plymouth Rock,
Massachusetts, he traveled the United States, visiting sites associ-
ated with "the New World" to separate reality from marketing.
Horowitz offers a fascinating look at organized historic spectacle.

Fieldwork Exercise Three

Get to know the history of the place where you're based. When was it
founded or first inhabited? Identify important historical markers. Are

there descriptions or maps of its earlier landscape? Focus on one time period. Interview someone connected to it—an eyewitness, a historian, a descendant of people who were there at the time. Think of Mother Tatiana, the Orthodox nun Robert Kaplan met in Serbia. Then write a short piece, three or four pages, blending the history you learned with the interview and the human persona of your source.

CRAFT DISCUSSION: SCENE AND SUMMARY

Francine Prose believes that young writers are sometimes too focused on "show, don't tell," leading to an overemphasis on scenes. We're in the room, on the boat, at the edge of the cliff, watching and feeling the character's experience. Scenes create the foreground and a sense of immediacy. But summaries offer background and context: Why is she in that closed room or boat in a storm? What brought him to that cliff? We need the backstory to clarify and help drive the narrative.

Scene and summary are sometimes described through the visual metaphor of a camera. Scenes focus through the zoom lens, creating close-up portraits that depend on detail, dialogue, and sensory perception. In chapter 2 we cited examples from Ernestine McHugh's *Love and Honor in the Himalayas* that show how dialogue rivets us to a specific time and place. We hear McHugh and her new mother speak; we feel the bond, smell the smoke of their shared cigarette. Creating dialogue can be tricky, as we discussed in chapter 5. If you don't have a recorded story and transcript, you must rely on memory. In creative nonfiction, re-creating dialogue is accepted practice. But that doesn't mean you can "make things up" like a fiction writer. You must struggle for the truth of what you remember. When in doubt, tell the reader you're uncertain, prefacing a segment with "I imagine it was like this" or "Maybe we set out at dawn, though it might have been later . . ."

Summary, in contrast, is "exposition" from the root word "to expose"—to reveal information about something, to explain or analyze. Unlike scenes, which re-create the experience in a sensory way, exposition *tells*. Saying "I stand at the entrance to the Reina Sophia Museum, the February wind and rain lashing my face . . ." places us. We feel the slap of the wet wind as we enter the museum at a specific moment. "I went to Spain because I wanted to see *Guernica*, the painting by Picasso that had shaped my life" begins the story of the author's longing. In summary, the writer can collapse huge segments of time into a paragraph or two.

D. J. Lee's essay "The Edge Is What We Have," about hiking the Grand Canyon with her father Denny, provides a useful example of a writer working between scene and summary. In backstory, Lee writes of her teenage years when her father wanted to expel her from the house for wild behavior. Lee's mother intervened, and in the end "he didn't make me go, but I knew that my place in the family was on shaky ground and that I had better turn things around." This backstory summarizes their difficult relationship in the past, setting up the present tense scenes, which track father and daughter on a hike through the canyon. The essay peaks when they find themselves unexpectedly walking a dangerous cliff trail: "I step on a loose piece of sandstone and my foot slips. I stop, frozen, staring at the ground. . . . Down there—who knows how far . . . a thousand feet? sits a raft . . . it looks like a child's bath toy. . . . I glance up. Denny has pitched himself against the bluff."[23]

The urgency of the situation is palpable. But scene would not carry much emotional weight without the background summary that developed the characters and complexity of the father-daughter relationship.

In similar fashion, in *The Devil's Highway*, Luis Alberto Urrea weaves scene and backstory throughout, keeping human character and history in tight proximity so each builds on the other. Urrea opens the book with a brutally visceral scene of five men crossing from Mexico into the United States. They "stumbled out of a mountain pass so sunstruck they didn't know their names." The reader feels the heat and thirst. "They whispered to each other as they staggered into parched pools of their own shadows." After a couple of pages the narrative moves into summary with a visual and historical sense of the geography the men are crossing, the Devil's Highway of the Cabeza Prieta Wilderness in Arizona. Urrea calls it "a vast trickery of sand," where the first recorded European "to die in the desert heat here did it on January 18, 1541."[24]

REVISION

Scenes and summary segments offers ample opportunities for revision. Often, you can expand or enliven a piece by adding a scene or clarify the backstory by inserting summary sections. Sometimes, a simple reordering is what's needed.

Revision Exercise One
Choose one of your freewrites from this chapter, perhaps something about a border crossing. Go back and write that material as a scene in the present tense, "I stand at the border of . . ." Then write a summary page giving us the backstory of how you got there and whatever a reader needs to know.

Our views of a place evolve over time, even within a given day. If we're faithful to our journals and record everything, we can chart changes in the landscape as well as in ourselves.

Revision Exercise Two
Find another freewrite in your notebook recorded at a particular time, say a park you often visited in the afternoon. Go back in the early morning, again in the evening, and later at night (with a friend if safety is an issue). Note all the changes in light, the people present, every small shift.

Experiment with Form—a Historical Timeline

Write an essay experimenting with time. Choose a place important to your travels and historical research. If you were following Kaplan's Balkan journey, you might start with "In Kosovo today, I see . . ." Then choose a significant occurrence in the past such as the carving up of the Balkans after World War I. Follow with imagining the landscape during that time: "In 1918 this must have looked . . ." Then make a timeline of events that happened in the intervening time period and go back and write several different versions of how you imagine the landscape.

Ethnographer Nancy Scheper-Hughes reminds us of how intimately we come to know a place through our explorations:

The ethnographer, like the artist, is engaged in a special kind of vision quest through which a specific interpretation of the human condition, an entire sensibility, is forged. Our medium, our canvas, is "the field," a place both proximate and intimate (because we live some part of our lives there). . . . In the act of "writing culture," what emerges is always a highly subjective, partial, and fragmentary—but also deeply felt and personal— record of human lives based on eyewitness and testimony.[25]

Which is to say, the ethnographer, the careful writer, the observant traveler all must move beyond the border and get to know a culture deeply. Readers want writers to take them to unfamiliar places, or revisit the known, but always to reveal some aspect of a place no one else has shown them.

7

RELIGION, POLITICS,

AND HISTORY

In his essay, "The Incredible Buddha Boy," George Saunders journeys from skepticism to respect for a religious experience that challenged his comprehension. His subject is a fifteen-year-old boy in Nepal who meditated for seven months without food and water—"supposedly" writes Saunders, signaling his initial doubt. Many Nepalese believed that this meditating boy might resolve the conflict between the monarchy and the Maoist rebels. At first Saunders resisted the assignment. But after weeks of telling humorous Buddha Boy stories at cocktail parties, his curiosity grew. He took the job and headed to Nepal.

In the resulting essay, Saunders's tone alternates between light-hearted and serious. Here is his description of his translator: a "kindly, media-savvy twenty-three-year-old who looks like a Nepali Robert Downey Jr."[1] On the solemn side, he describes reaching the Buddha Boy's meditation site: "My mouth is dry, and I have a sudden feeling of gratitude/reverence/terror. What a privilege. Oh God, I have somehow underestimated the gravity of this place and moment. I am potentially at a great religious site, in the original mythic time: at Christ's manger, say, with Shakyamuni at Bodh Gaya, watching Moses come down from the Mount."[2] Saunders's emotional honesty and skilled storytelling carry us with him on the path from discomfort to new awareness.

Like Saunders, we all confront the limits of our understanding in new cultural settings. The realms of religion and politics can intensify our struggle. But if we write with respect about worlds we don't fully grasp, we can at least honor the questions.

RELIGION, VISION, AND EMPATHY

People in all societies create stories, rituals and beliefs to account for the nature of the sacred, for the mysteries of human existence, and to offer guidance on how to live. Religion may mean communion with nature at a Wicca event, participation in a Methodist service, or attendance at a Korean shaman's ritual. The sacred might include individual enlightenment on a pilgrimage or collective grieving at the death of a village elder.

Religion also offers remarkable insights into a culture. Nigeria, for example, honors the Yoruba deity Ogun—a god of road travel frequently invoked by writer Wole Soyinka. Ogun presides over change, movement, and risk—essential in a country with one of the world's highest auto accident rates. If you've done advance research, you'll know that what looks like a car wreck on the side of the road is actually a shrine to Ogun.

From the earliest pilgrims' stories through today's accounts, travel writers have recorded their reactions to religious experience. Many eighteenth- and nineteenth-century explorers described non-Christians as "primitive" or "heathen." Yet others chronicled their fascination and wonder at divergent belief systems. Lewis Henry Morgan, who pioneered kinship studies in the late nineteenth century, wrote detailed accounts of the religious practices of American Indian cultures. He probed the meaning of burial practices, beliefs about the soul, and relationships between humans and animals. His work "showed that anthropology was impossible without travel, and that travel literature in turn could and should take note of the anthropologist's approach to his subject."[3]

Many contemporary travel writers follow the lead of their more broad-minded predecessors. Some, like Saunders, balance an outward focus with personal revelations. In "The Incredible Buddha Boy," he describes joining a procession of pilgrims in prayer as they circle a Buddhist stupa. Saunders has had a rough year, he tells us: the destruction of his parents' house during Hurricane Katrina, a relative sent to fight in Iraq, and his realization that he may one day lose his beloved wife. All this leads to his pronouncement about the nature of being human: a being who, "having lived a while, becomes terrified and, having become terrified, deeply craves an end to the fear."[4] Saunders's use of the "I" is judicious. His repetition of "terrified" deepens the emotional impact. His disclosure is individual but transcends the merely personal. The reader feels the universality of despair, our shared craving for absolution and release from suffering.

Another writer who achieves internal growth via religious culture is Faith Adiele. She fled the United States for Thailand after she hit a crisis point, forced to choose between "black or white America, material or spiritual gain, gender or racial allegiance, beauty or safety, myself or others."[5] Wanting to "squat at the clash of cultures," she chose the punishing path of ordination as a Buddhist nun. Though she lived the role with fierce commitment, she found that what she learned had less to do with being Buddhist or a nun than with becoming "a new kind of traveler—the Hungry American—who set out in search of faith without a map."[6]

Religion often intersects with healing, a juncture where opposing beliefs can determine life or death. Anne Fadiman's *The Spirit Catches You and You Fall Down* recounts competing cultural interpretations of epilepsy and the tragic outcome for Lia Lee, a Hmong child in Merced, California. Fadiman juxtaposes two worldviews. While Western doctors consider epilepsy a neurological disorder, the Hmong view the illness as a special affliction with spiritual dimensions. She portrays the doctors and Lia's parents as equally caring and devoted to the child. The reader feels the humanity of everyone involved, rendering Lia's death even more tragic. Fadiman achieves this equilibrium by positioning herself to see all perspectives. She writes, "I have always felt that the action most worth watching is not at the center of things but where edges meet. I like shorelines, weather fronts, international borders. There are interesting frictions and incongruities in these places, and often, if you stand at the point of tangency, you can see both sides better than if you were in the middle of either one. This is especially true, I think, when the apposition is cultural."[7]

As you encounter unfamiliar religions and practices, try to stand at the edge and see multiple points of view. Examine your own ideas to see where conflicts and congruities emerge.

Writing Exercise One

To articulate your own thinking, begin a freewrite: "first thoughts on religion." Read local papers to augment prior research on which religions are dominant in the place where you're living. Then, walk the streets and record the names of churches, synagogues, mosques, or any structure that might be considered religious. Your list might include places like Alcoholics Anonymous meeting centers. Many people consider Alcoholics Anonymous and similar groups to be religious for their adherence to a higher power.

Sometimes, penetrating unfamiliar beliefs require a leap beyond logic. For polyglot writer Elias Canetti, confusion turned to empathy after a visit to Morocco. The blind beggars and their chants of "Allah" had mesmerized him in the markets of Marrakesh. He wanted to get beyond formal language and let the sounds physically enter him. "The blind," he wrote, "offer one the name of God, and by giving alms one can acquire a claim on him. They begin with God, they end with God, they repeat God's name ten thousand times a day." Back from Morocco, still haunted, Canetti sat down, closed his eyes, and sat in the corner of his room repeating "Alláh! Alláh! Alláh!" over and over again. "I tried to imagine myself going on saying it for a whole day and a large part of the night; taking a short sleep and then beginning again; doing the same thing for days and weeks, months and years; growing old and older and living like that." Canetti came to realize that there are realms "beyond words, deeper and more equivocal than words."[8]

George Saunders also registers a physical reaction when he finally meets the Buddha Boy. He describes him with short, staccato words and phrases: "His quality of nonmotion is startling. His head doesn't move. His arms, hands, don't move. Nothing moves. . . . He could be dead. . . . His hands are in one of the mudras in which the Buddha's hands are traditionally depicted. He is absolutely beautiful. . . . My heart rate is going through the roof."[9]

Canetti and Saunders struggled to empathize with unknown worlds through observation and imaginative projection. Documentary photographer Dorothea Lange often gave her students an assignment with a similar agenda: to build empathy and teach them to see differently. She instructed them to watch passersby on the street, then invent biographies for the people they observed—a creative exercise but one based on disciplined attention. Students might assume that the woman in a fashionable suit had an office job or the man in overalls worked construction. But even if proved wrong, they'd uncover their biases and move toward greater understanding.

✔

Writing Exercise Two

Choose an event related to religious belief that you didn't or still don't understand. Describe it in a scene, using the first person to record what you saw and experienced. Then describe in the third person what you imagine a participant in that world might have experienced. Make clear to the reader that you are speculating. You could begin "I can't know but I imagine that . . ."

POLITICS AND BEYOND

"Politics" comes from the Greek, *politikos*, "of, for, or relating to citizens." Politics concerns how people govern and exercise power. In the public realm, power may play out in the courthouse of a nation-state or the tribal council in a traditional community. In rural or urban settings, you might begin to explore whatever public arena is available—a community center in a Kenyan village, a town hall in Norway, a city council meeting in Sydney. Walk the streets or pathways. Note political slogans on walls and eavesdrop in cafés where people gather. Read and listen to the news. Record or clip stories that awaken your interest even if you don't yet understand the context. In your journal, remember to be inclusive, noting things that may seem outside politics. We can't know in advance what might be relevant later.

Essayist Leslie Jamison shows how issues of power permeate daily life. While in Bolivia, she picked up the newspaper *Correo del Sur* in a grocery store. Ads for sex services appeared on the "personals" page: "Janeth offers 'servicio supercompleta con una señorita superatractiva.'" Two months later, Jamison found a story in the same paper about a group of sex workers on strike in a city near La Paz. She wrote, "The bars and brothels where these women worked had been vandalized. They sat in protest for days outside a local health clinic. *Servicios supercompletas.* They sewed their lips together with thread."[10] The impact of Jamison's story comes from the repetition of "servicios supercompletas" in different contexts and from the juxtaposition of mundane and horrifying details. Jamison also forces the reader to face a brutal truth about politics, power, and travel: people's lives demand our attention, but we may lack the means to do much beyond witness.

Gender politics have always shaped women's travel experience. In chapter 1, we noted the work of Isabelle Eberhardt, who dressed as a man to live more freely in Algeria. But women travelers also have advantages. They can enter worlds closed to their male counterparts, opening up alternative views of the "political." Imagine you're in a country where women's access to public spaces is forbidden or curtailed. The home, the beauty salon, the segregated schoolroom may be the best places to observe power held by women. Sometimes, communication from disempowered groups emerges in surprising ways. In India, Greece, and Ireland, women traditionally perform lament poetry for the dead. But sometimes their expressions convey other, forbidden messages. Irish writer and folklorist Angela Bourke details how women's laments, called "keening" in Ireland, vented anger at public figures who abused power or at husbands who drank. The Irish government and Catholic Church both tried to suppress keening.[11] You might turn to folklore such as songs or oral stories to find these hidden dimensions of power.

Groups forced underground in some cultures, such as gay, lesbian, bisexual, or transgender (LGBT) residents, may also have to cloak their communications. Throughout history, many LGBT travelers have hidden their identities. But recent publications such as Michael T. Luongo's collection of essays, *Gay Travels in the Muslim World*, suggest a shift. In the book's introduction, Luongo probes the complex post-9/11 links between fears of terrorism, Muslims, and gays. His wide-ranging collection, which includes the story of a gay soldier in Iraq, refutes simplistic ideas about Muslims or gays. Jay Davidson, for example, a "nice Jewish boy," recounts his time as a Peace Corps volunteer in Mauritania. After his first romantic encounter, his new partner becomes infatuated with a female volunteer, overturning Davidson's hopes and assumptions. He sums up what he learned—a useful guide for anyone living abroad: "If a society's culture is a mosaic of thousands of little tiles, then I like to think that what I have been able to piece together has been a tableau in which certain aspects have become discernable, some are a little less clear, and others remain in a way that I will never see as whole and comprehensible."[12]

Writing Exercise Three

Freewrite your first thoughts on "politics." Then describe a scene you've witnessed that might be considered political. If possible, compare public and private settings to explore what counts as power.

Travelers often wrestle with tension between their own experience and the broad social issues they encounter. In a culture where people lack shoes, should you gripe about your blistered feet? Yet we need to record changes within as well as beyond ourselves. Sometimes a literary structure provides a way to show both. In her biography of journalist Josephine Herbst, Elinor Langer describes her subject's double consciousness while in Cuba in 1935. Herbst was on assignment for the *American Mercury* to cover the political upheaval exacerbated by U.S. business interests. She had just separated from her husband, John Herrmann. While she awaited an introduction to the revolutionary underground, Herbst fought loneliness and despair. Langer juxtaposes excerpts from Herbst's letters to her husband with notes on Cuban politics and economics to display her subject's divided self. Much of the chapter looks like this:

From the Letters:	*From the Notes:*
Am writing this in a café. . . . You have been flooded with letters from me, far too many. I can't understand why I haven't had a letter from you. I know I see it all in a crazy unreal haze but I can't help that. I wouldn't mind not hearing if we'd parted in an ordinary way but after all, John darling, we didn't.	Sugar. 80% of sugar industry belongs to US citizens, balance controlled largely by Am. creditors. Tobacco same. Banks, railroads, streetcar lines, . . . and other utilities owned by US capital.[13]

———————————————— ✔ ————————————————

Writing Exercise Four

In your journal, keep a page for political events recorded from the daily paper, the Internet, or observed on the street. On a facing page, keep track of your internal world, charting the full range of emotion. Use short descriptions, as Herbst did. You can develop these ideas later.

———————————————————————————————————————

A caveat about political life: in some parts of the world, foreigners risk arrest or worse when they participate in protests, meetings, or rallies or even express opinions publicly. Host institutions may prohibit visitors from attending or documenting political events. Even journalists with an internationally recognized press pass can be denied access and face danger. Before you attend a meeting or public protest, research the legal and ethical consequences. List possible risks. It's easy, even with the best planning, to get caught up in something you did not foresee.

RITUALS: SECULAR AND SACRED

Rituals in every culture help make sense of our lives. Rites of passage, delineated in the early twentieth century by French ethnographer Arnold Van Gennep, mark transitions from one stage of life to another—birth ceremonies, weddings, graduations, funerals, and others. Many rituals gather families and communities in annual commemoration, marking time's passage. Think of Thanksgiving or the spring revelry of Holi, when streets in India and Nepal run red and orange with colored water. Rituals also hold up what anthropologist Barbara Myerhoff called "cultural mirrors." When Mexicans make the pilgrimage to the Basilica of Our Lady of Guadalupe—Basílica de Nuestra Señora de Guadalupe—they see their complex mix of indigenous and European cultures in the brown-skinned Virgin.

Rituals can be secular—a football game or Halloween viewing of *The Rocky Horror Picture Show*—or sacred—a Catholic mass, Jewish bar or bat mitzvah, the pilgrimage to Mecca, or a shaman's ceremony. You might document a rally of the Labor Party faithful in Australia, then turn to an Aboriginal ceremony or a Greek Orthodox service. Most rituals follow a sequence of events performed in a prescribed way, using symbols, gestures, words, and objects.

As noted in chapter 6 about historical reenactments, some rituals feel homegrown while others seem staged for outsiders. Imagine you're in Seville, where you suddenly hear the thunder of clapping hands. Down a side street, you discover a flamenco guitarist, a dancer, and a gaggle of bar patrons spilled out into the street. Two weeks later, you attend a flamenco concert in a tourist venue. Both are electrifying performances. One is obviously more spontaneous, the other professionally staged. But is one more "authentic"? Our search for culture in its "natural" state, writes Dean MacCannell in *The Tourist*, is part of modernity. "For moderns, reality and authenticity are thought to be elsewhere: in other historical periods and other cultures, in purer, simpler lifestyles."[14]

Rituals also shift over time, sometimes to accommodate outsiders. Take American Indian powwows, essential to indigenous communities since nineteenth-century intertribal gatherings on the plains. Today, the dancing, drumming, and singing may happen on college campuses and in urban settings as well as on reservations. W. Richard West Jr., founding director of the National Museum of the American Indian, stresses that contemporary powwows rectify the "dog days of adverse Indian policy" when the U.S. government terminated tribes and nearly destroyed aspects of indigenous cultures. Outsiders can serve as witnesses to the ongoing power of powwows as a "potent cultural and social connector among contemporary Indian communities."[15] Whether such events are "authentic" is ultimately a community decision and designation.

✔

Fieldwork Exercise One

Make a list of rituals, secular and sacred, in this new place. Attend one, either a public event or a private one to which you are invited. Carry a small notebook to make notes on the physical layout, who participates, when it occurs, and the sequence of events. Freewrite later on what you saw, felt, and heard. If possible, follow up by interviewing one or more participants. Why do they attend? Has the ritual changed over time and how do they feel about those shifts?

HISTORICAL RESEARCH AND IMAGINATION

Historical research can illuminate the contemporary scene, especially via contrast. George Saunders introduces Katmandu in "The Incredible Buddha Boy" by showing how the past lingers in the present. The absence of streetlights, he tells us, makes Katmandu appear like a medieval city, as if "the cab has been time-transported back to the age of kings and squalor, and we are making our way through the squalor to the palace, which is now the Hyatt."[16] Saunders's characteristic humor quickly turns more serious when he describes the stupa that dates back to 500 A.D. He creates a timeline during which thousands have circumambulated this stupa during "Shakespeare's time, while Washington lived, during the Civil War, as Glenn Miller played."[17]

A search for the past might extend beyond formal archives and libraries to dusty attics, local museums, the back of general stores, police stations, churches, and town halls. Don't overlook these potential treasure troves because they're not official. Sometimes the most interesting archival material has been papered over or otherwise hidden. In the Vosges Mountains of France, on the German border, people still find graffiti carved into rocks by lonely German sentries during World War I.

Many historians now mine such "unofficial" sources. The Annales School, a movement begun by twentieth-century French
historians, investigates history using social science methods—a bit
like an ethnographer viewing the past as a foreign country. *The
Return of Martin Guerre* was a popular 1982 film based on the book
by Annales scholar Natalie Zemon Davis. She scoured judicial records, tax rolls, early pamphlets, and folktales to research this story
of sixteenth-century identity theft in a French village.

In Joanne's experience with Alutiiq communities on Kodiak
Island, Alaska, in the 1970s, many people housed valuable artifacts
such as painted hunting hats and sealskin parkas in their attics. For
decades, Alaska Natives had feared bringing such articles to public
attention since their culture had been derided as "bastardized" or
destroyed by outsiders. But after a twenty-year period of cultural
revitalization, many of those objects now rest in Kodiak's Alutiiq
Museum. Context, historical shifts, and issues of power all influence what is regarded as official or valuable.

Oral histories complement archival research. Objects and photos are useful prompts during interviews to uncover attitudes toward local or national history. As we discussed in chapter 4, oral
histories reflect what people believe as well as what they know to
be factual. Some stories are reshaped in the telling about events,
becoming mythic in collective memory.

Fieldwork Exercise Two
Return to the ritual event you attended or choose a new site. Perhaps you
visited a Shinto shrine while living with a family in Japan. Now follow
up with researching websites, libraries, and archives on the history of
Shinto rituals and beliefs. Write a three-page overview. Include a bibli-
ography of your primary and secondary sources.

Graveyards disclose as much about the living as the dead. How a group honors the deceased, decorates and maintains graves, and chooses where to bury people all uncover past and present values. Graves are often segregated by race, ethnicity, religion, or other social markers. Now, communities with large immigrant populations in the United States, Australia, and parts of Europe must integrate new ideas about death and burials. Turkish American Osman Balkan studied the cultural clash over burials between Germans and Turkish immigrants to that country. Balkan trailed and interviewed Muslim undertakers whom he describes as "cultural brokers" with a nearly religious authority because of their proximity to death. They must negotiate a labyrinth of German bureaucratic rules, including the requisite forty-eight-hour waiting period before burial. Islam, in contrast, mandates that bodies be immediately interred and face Mecca, a challenge with Germany's limited cemetery space. Where and how to bury a body is a practical matter, Balkan writes, but burials pose a deeper, more enduring question: "You ask yourselves as a people, 'Who are we? Where is home?'"[18]

Fieldwork Exercise Three

Make a map of the local burial grounds, seeking permission if needed. Are the graves divided by religion? Ethnicity? Do infants have a special place? Record the type of gravestones, other burial markers such as photos and flowers, epitaphs, names, and dates. Write a scene of your experience in the graveyard and what you observed.

NAMES, LABELS, AND CATEGORIES

In *Writing the Memoir: From Truth to Art*, Judith Barrington discusses the power of names to enliven your writing. Throughout the book, we have stressed a focus on details. But names and labels can also create rigid categories that inhibit understanding. Consider "Republican," "Libertarian," or "Democrat" in the United States and the autoresponse each generates. Or compare how and when "terrorist" appears in the *New York Times* or the *Washington Post* versus *Arab News* (www.arabnews.com). Sometimes we internalize political terms as natural categories. Think about the transformation of "Christian Democracy." Born in nineteenth-century Europe, this party originally combined conservative politics and Catholic social policy, even as it branched out to other continents. The party's ideological framework has remained fairly conservative and center-right in Europe, while shifting to the left in Latin America.

How will you discover the culturally appropriate terms for different groups? In the United States, various indigenous groups prefer "Native American" to "Indian," while "Alaska Natives" encompasses the state's diverse people. Some Mexican Americans choose "Latino" or "Chicano" over "Hispanic." These terms unveil political and social categories and their history. Interviews can aid the learning process. How and why do people choose a particular affiliation or terminology? Do they follow their parents' path or change allegiance under the sway of friends or teachers? When we write, we may reinforce existing categories by the words we choose, our syntax, and other aspects of language. Think about passive voice in historical writing. Actors can escape the consequences of their actions, as in descriptions of slavery in some U.S. textbooks. Try describing what you observe in a culture without names or labels. Because our reliance on naming is often unconscious, this can be more difficult than you think.

Writing Exercise Five

Choose one of the rituals you witnessed and wrote about. Go back and strip out every label or category that might be considered religious or political. Describe the events as though you were speaking to someone from an alien world who had no concept of Hindu or Jewish or Socialist. Revise and clarify what remains, then freewrite on what you learned.

POLITICS, CULTURE, AND ETHICAL CHOICES

Abroad, ethical choices may be magnified. If you feel strongly about any topic, you will likely confront behavior somewhere in the world that will rile you. For a Western feminist, it may be the greater freedom men enjoy in some places or practices such as female circumcision. The people you view as offenders may consider themselves feminists or progressives or conservatives, too, but based on different criteria. You may hear racist or discriminatory language justified by the speakers as "part of our culture." How do you weigh cultural relativism against broader human rights? In an interview in the 1990s, anthropologist Clifford Geertz stressed, "Understanding what people think doesn't mean you have to think the same thing." Human conflict isn't simply a clash of ideas. "There are people attached to those ideas. If you want to live without violence, you have to realize that other people are as real as you are."[19]

Should you voice your beliefs to new friends or host families? Boycott events? The environmental movement has garnered worldwide support as we face global crises from water shortages to endangered species. In many places, greed drives poaching and exploitation of resources. But so does poverty. How does your social position affect your judgment? The complexity of each situation may tax your beliefs.

Imagine you're invited to a bullfight in Spain. You recoil at the violence. Yet you want to understand the critical importance of bullfighting, which appears not on the sports page of *El País* but in the culture section. What does it mean to attend? To not attend? Maybe forgo the bullfight but talk with a variety of Spaniards about their views. Interview both sides, placing the words of a *torero* alongside those of an anti-bullfight activist. Understanding comes from the willingness to suspend judgment and commit time to observation, research, and writing.

Death without Weeping, Nancy Scheper-Hughes's powerful account of life in the Brazilian shantytown of Bom Jesus de Mata, provides a good example of in-depth participant observation and nuanced writing. Scheper-Hughes balances anthropological distance with emotional outrage at the poverty that drives mothers' "selective neglect" (also sometimes called "passive infanticide"). In the following example, she presents multiple points of view. First we meet Nailza, a woman who has just lost a baby girl, Joana, a "little angel gone to heaven." At night Scheper-Hughes hears Nailza's angry conversations with the dead child: "Why did you leave me? Was your patron saint so greedy that she would not allow me one child on this earth?"[20] Another woman explains to Scheper-Hughes that this is a normal kind of madness that will fade. Indeed, we soon learn that "the premature birth of a stillborn son" some months later "cured" Nailza of her "inappropriate" grief. Scheper-Hughes's ironic use of quotation marks reveals her own attitudes but she uses the voices of women to show us the logic of beliefs born of impoverishment.

Though you may still find certain cultural practices irksome or incomprehensible, if you've tried to see another point of view, you will have met important criteria for an ethical traveler.

Writing Exercise Six

Choose a political issue or a religious or cultural belief or practice to which you had a negative reaction. Freewrite your first thoughts, giving full rein to your disapproval, doubts, and discomfort. Then go back and write as a believer, starting with "If I were a [man, woman, child] in this culture, perhaps I too might [attend bullfights, eat raw meat, walk to a pilgrimage site on my knees, etc.] . . ." Incorporate research on the meaning of these beliefs or practices.

CRAFT DISCUSSION: INTEGRATING
BACKGROUND MATERIAL

As discussed in chapter 6, scene and summary are both essential to nonfiction. Scenes use imagery, dialogue, and dramatic enactments. They condense time. Summaries provide information, data, and backstory. They expand time, often slowing the pace of a story. But how can a writer integrate background on the Ottoman Empire or Uruguayan politics without an "information dump" that bores the reader?

In *Crescent and Star: Turkey between Two Worlds*, Stephen Kinzer skillfully fuses information with story. He opens a chapter on the Kurds with a scene. A respected old man in the Diyarbakir Bazaar sits on a beat-up couch recounting to Kinzer his memories of the Kurds' struggle. "'Even though it's dangerous for me to say this, I have been greatly oppressed in my lifetime,' he told me as he leaned his chin on his wooden cane. 'I have been tortured many times.'"[21] Nearby sits a group of teenagers, gripped by a story that will ignite their own activism. The arresting scene brings the present into focus before Kinzer turns to the past.

"The Kurdish conflict is Turkey's festering wound, and to travel to Diyarbakir and from there through eastern provinces where Kurds constitute the large majority is to see the country's ugliest face. . . . For thousands of years Kurds have lived in what used to be called Mesopotamia and what some now call Kurdistan, a name the Turkish government rejects because of its supposed political taint."[22] Kinzer travels back further, telescoping thousands of years of history. He quotes the fourth century B.C. Greek commander Xenophon who described the Kurds' warlike and rebellious character. When Kinzer concludes that Kurds never submit to anyone, we believe him. We've heard the history. We've sat with the contemporary version of a Kurdish warrior. In this brief segment, Kinzer creates a strong sense of place through a scene and a feeling for a people through a summary of their history.

Writing Exercise Seven

Choose a scene from your notes on the ritual you attended, let's say the Shinto shrine. Begin a freewrite with the prompt, "Here's a contemporary scene . . ." Describe what you witnessed in detail, incorporating dialogue between participants. In fieldwork exercise 2, you did historical research on that ritual. Start a new paragraph with "To understand this scene today, you need to know that . . ." and blend in that material.

REVISION

After spending time in a culture, your political or religious practices or beliefs may be validated or shaken. What matters is that you stayed open to either possibility. Revising first thoughts and impressions can chart how far you've traveled.

Revision Exercise One

Return to your first thoughts on politics and religion. Has your initial understanding changed? Do a new freewrite starting with "On further thought, I think that . . ." If your thinking hasn't shifted, follow with "I still don't understand . . ." Or "I now more firmly believe . . ."

Revision Exercise Two

Survey the journal notes where you juxtaposed two columns: personal reactions versus observations of the political/social realm. Write an essay melding the two.

Experiment with Form—Comparison/Contrast

Sometimes the simplest structures achieve complexity. One basic essay form is comparison/contrast. Sometimes, that structure invites a writer to play with time. In her essay "Two Baths," Elizabeth Graver begins, "I was, at this first bath, [at age] twenty, spending the year studying in France but traveling for a week with an American friend in Germany." The next section, set off by the number "2," opens, "And then I was thirty . . ."[23] Graver travels with her mother in Turkey, then moves around in time and place, ending at a Turkish bath. Along the way, she explores her Jewish identity, German history and the Holocaust, her grandmother's life as a Sephardic Jew in Istanbul, and a great many other topics. The simple two-part structure allows her to roam yet keep the reader grounded in a compelling tale.

You can use this two-part structure in different ways. One possibility is to choose an event or place you experienced more than once. Following Graver, explore two encounters, beginning each with a scene. Or shape an essay around dual perspectives. As suggested in other exercises, you could interview a community member on a controversial topic, then find someone who sees the other side. Transcribe the recordings. Juxtapose the views, starting the essay with: "Here's one truth . . ." Begin part two with "Here's another perspective . . ."

Writer Mohsin Hamid once compared religious practice to writing fiction. His views are useful for the nonfiction writer as well: "Writing fiction is, in many ways, like a religion. It is a daily practice, a way of life, a set of rituals, an orientation toward the universe. It is a communion with the intangible, a bridge between the finite and infinite. There's a reason religions use stories to communicate, and it's the same reason religions persecute storytellers: Stories are powerful. They are how we make sense of what cannot be known."[24]

George Saunders ends his essay on the Buddha Boy with the news he received two months after his return to the United States. The boy disappeared, rumors abounded. About a week later, the BBC reported that the boy had met with the Village Committee. He declared that he was headed back into hiding, and promised to reappear in six years. Saunders conjures the night of the boy's escape into the forest, "his eyes really open for the first time since May. The world, the beautiful world, is fleeting past, and he's seeing it in a way we can't imagine. He's come so far and is desperate to get somewhere beyond the reach of the world, so he can finish what he's started. He hasn't eaten in ten months, and isn't hungry."[25] In the end, Saunders can only bow to the mystery.

8

TRAVEL WRITING IN

THE AGE OF THE INTERNET

Hurricane Sandy, the storm that hit the United States east coast on October 29, 2012, may not be an obvious event to open a chapter on travel writing and social media. But during the storm, Facebook and Twitter helped people survive across a devastated landscape, proving social media's ability to record history, exchange raw information, and establish event chronologies in real time. That kind of techno-logical edge can be helpful while on the road and doing research. Of course, social media feeds aren't screened by professional editors, and thus don't benefit from fact-checking and editing. This doesn't stop active users from jumping on errors, such as basic grammar or perceived errors in fact. Yet during Sandy's worst hours, Twitter brought people together to share information on services, transport, medical care, and shelter. In other words, for many people Twitter became an electronic savior in a natural disaster.

A few days after the storm, Pietro Rea, a tech blogger for the *Huffington Post* who rode out the hurricane in his New York City apartment, wrote: "I needed something that was fast and to the point. Do I have to evacuate? Cool. Did my neighbor's building just collapse? Got it."[1] During the storm, more than twenty million Tweets were recorded from people caught in the area. Thanks to Twitter, we have a strong street-level sense of what was happening in the areas Sandy hit hardest—an unfiltered, uncensored record of what people felt, what they saw, and how they coped.

Similar scenes have unfolded around the world. In Tunisia and Egypt, countries that touched off the Arab Spring that swept North Africa and the Middle East in 2011, first Facebook and then Twitter proved invaluable to populist forces galvanizing support. This is true as well for protests connected to the Occupy Wall Street movement.

Travel writing has entered a new age where information access and communication can also connect people and increase potential audiences for our writing. Technology can make travel easier and more spontaneous but also more shallow. Well-known travel writers like Paul Theroux and Robert Kaplan, among others, have denounced how e-mail, cell phones, and social media cheapen the experience of getting out of town. The ease of connection with home can distract travelers from the rich culture around them.

In 2012, Kaplan, a national correspondent for the *Atlantic Monthly*, wrote: "I get off a 15-hour flight from North America and turn on my BlackBerry at some Asian airport. Instead of focusing on the immediate environment . . . I am engrossed in the several dozen e-mails that piled up while I was en route." Kaplan argues, "The intensity of the experience of foreign places has been diluted."[2] Paul Theroux put it this way in a 2012 interview with Salon.com: "I can tell you from experience that being in central Africa without any contact with the outside world forces you to learn the language, make friends and live with the people. You return to yourself. But if you have an iPad, you have weather reports, the news, and a spouse or friend at the other end."[3]

Kaplan's and Theroux's concerns are valid, but for better or worse social media is here to stay and evolving rapidly. The social media universe includes blogs, "microblogs" like Twitter, networking sites such as Facebook, content communities such as YouTube and Instagram, and virtual social worlds of all kinds. By the time this book goes to press, there will certainly be new social media sites out there with fresh innovations we have not considered. Twitter is already losing ground, though Facebook is stronger than ever. You may not use either of these, but chances are you're linked to people you know through some kind of technology. The trick is to learn to use these forms without sacrificing experiences that teach us how to adapt to new places. It might be more helpful to think of social media as a tool that enhances the coping process in a crisis, like the way Pietro Rea used Twitter to gather information on what was happening in his neighborhood during a hurricane.

We also need to honor other cultural values about technology. As you travel, you'll encounter different attitudes toward social media depending on the country, its religious practices, and other aspects of culture. Even within the United States, some religions forbid use of e-mail and Facebook at certain times, such as the Jewish Sabbath. Don't assume that because an African farmer has a cell phone and his son has a Facebook page that their values match yours. Recently the *New York Times* reported how tourists around the world abuse social media and violate sensitivities in countries they visit, sometimes even physically harming cultural sites. In March 2015, two California women were arrested after carving their initials into the wall of the Colosseum in Rome for a picture. "From posing naked at Machu Picchu to filming their dives from hotel balconies into courtyard swimming pools," the *Times* reported, "travelers across the world have been indulging in what officials and travel experts describe as an epidemic of narcissism and recklessness, as they try to turn vacation hubs and historic sites into their personal video and photography props."[4] Such offenders represent all nationalities but, thankfully, only a minority of travelers.

Even if you're savvy about all forms of social media, we want to urge you to consider how strong writing can enhance your profile. Your travel Tweets, Facebook posts, blogs, and other posts should be sharp, crisp, honest, clear, and memorable. The Nigerian writer Teju Cole (now living in New York) is a good example of a writer creatively engaged with Twitter. He uses the medium to post observations, favorite lines of poetry, and his own poetry and brief articles. Consider Cole's Twitter essay on the Nigerian terror group, Boko Haram, and the April 2014 kidnapping of some two hundred schoolgirls. Cole's first post in the series reads, "Terrorism is not a natural disaster." The series continues for more than sixty posts, including maps.[5]

In this book our focus is writing and travel, not technology, but we encourage a happy marriage of the two. We'll limit the social media discussion to Twitter, Facebook, and longer forms such as blogging. It's up to you to choose the social media that works best for you.

POPULAR FORMS OF SOCIAL MEDIA: TWITTER VERSUS FACEBOOK

Facebook is almost as widely used in developing countries as the cell phone. You can Tweet and post on Facebook as easily from the West African countryside as you can from southern Idaho. Because Facebook's audience is limited by privacy settings as well as by handpicked "friends," the writer can create a particular audience. This influences the content, style, and frequency of posts. Unlike Twitter, Facebook posts can be as long as needed. Facebook can also be abused. Despite many such examples, Facebook still serves a wide and growing readership.

Twitter posts move more quickly, with fewer limitations as to audience, creating different possibilities and problems. Tweets are far more exposed than Facebook, unless you adjust your Twitter settings so that only your followers see your posts. Otherwise, Tweets go out to everyone with Internet access, depending on the subjects of interest. With Facebook or Twitter, your writing can have unexpected consequences. Media law expert Mark Pearson details the legal and security risks of social media. "Every time an

internet user blogs or Tweets," Pearson writes, "they may be subject to the laws of more than 200 jurisdictions. As more than a few
bloggers or Tweeters have discovered, you can be sued in your own
country, or arrested in a foreign airport as you're heading off on
vacation—just for writing something that wouldn't raise an eye-
brow if you said it in a bar or a cafe."[6]

More problems potentially arise as people misinterpret a Facebook post or a Tweet or when people don't appreciate your attempt at humor. There are now hundreds, maybe thousands of
online examples of thoughtless posts that have gotten social media
users in trouble, such as the Facebook user who was arrested for an
offhand joke about gunplay. In Turkey, police have arrested both
Turks and foreigners for social media posts deemed politically or
culturally offensive.

Since Tweets condense thought to 140 characters, this form
demands succinct writing—a skill valuable in many genres. Such
brevity represents a superb challenge: how to distill an idea, observation, or question to its essence in a way that is sharp and clear,
almost like a newspaper lede paragraph. As always with your writing, avoid already covered subjects. Be fresh. Focus on the ironic,
the odd, the unreported.

The speed of social media can make you forget essentials of
grammar and punctuation. But these remain essential. Use of active
verbs will help you cut adjectives and adverbs. (See chapter 9 for an
expanded discussion of revision and editing.) You'll save space and
your Tweets will read more energetically. A good set of guidelines
for writing Twitter posts can be found at the AdWeek website.[7]

As of this writing, a check of Twitter feeds in Thailand (https://
twitter.com/hashtag/thailand) reveal a host of information, from
places to eat and tourist attractions, to evolving political crises. Scanning the posts, you can judge which posts are more effective. Look
for clear, interesting writing on intriguing subjects, such as this post
about the plight of migrant children in Thailand: "While I was sleeping, a rat bit my face."[8] You can also check Yelp and TripAdvisor for
advice on practical matters, but Tweets cover a vast range of topics.

Writing Exercise One

Read through your journal and pull out a story of something you'd like to share with others in a Tweet. Whittle it down, focusing on sensory details. Write three Tweets from your journal entries, eliminating the verb "to be" and unnecessary adverbs and adjectives. Share with a group of readers before you send. It's easy to slam out a Tweet. So, before you do, consider its accuracy and potential impact. Are there consequences you might not have thought about? If you are unsure, those readers might save you some embarrassment.

Poets, especially writers of the haiku and the sonnet, might say the Tweet is nothing new, a short writing form that people have been trying to master for centuries. Perhaps the same can be said for Facebook posts, the vast majority of which are short status updates. Voltaire, the eighteenth-century French poet, philosopher, and historian, offered an early definition of the Tweet when he said that poetry "says more and in fewer words than prose."[9] More recently, the writer Salman Rushdie best summed up the job of the poet: "A poet's work is to name the unnamable, to point at frauds, to take sides, start arguments, shape the world, and stop it going to sleep." The same could be said of the Tweeter. Rushdie happens to be an avid Tweeter. In a December 2013 Tweet, for example, Rushdie wrote: "Sunday thought. The books we love change how we see the world. For me it all began with Alice in Wonderland. What books changed you?"[10]

Writing Exercise Two

Choose a Tweet or Facebook post of yours about something you observed, like the taxi driver who told you the story of his daughter's divorce. You fired off a quick Tweet or short paragraph on Facebook about the experience. Now turn what you wrote into a haiku by cutting it all down to seventeen syllables over three lines: five, seven, and five syllables, respectively. Then do the inverse, jotting down notes as you take a walk, for example, later turning them into haikus, and, finally, revising the notes into Tweets. What are the advantages of each form?

If you discipline yourself to develop an economy of language, you'll learn to pack a lot into 140 characters. This kind of discipline might also make your Facebook posts more concise and meaningful. During a month-long trip, if you send two or three Tweets a day, you will have a chronological record of your travels and experiences. Your social media posts can complement your more detailed journal and also create digital maps of where you've been. All Tweets, like Facebook posts, are automatically dated with a time stamp. You can mark each with a place or dateline, like a regular journal entry.

So, go forth and post but be choosy about what you send. Keep it interesting.

FIRST THOUGHTS AND JOURNALS

As we've discussed, when recording first impressions, it's important to strip away your filters and write down fears, prejudices, and every range of emotion. Later, you'll measure shifts in feeling. But social media as a form of journaling must be carefully edited. It's tempting to type something quickly and hit "send." Many of us know the pain of such mistakes from using e-mail. As discussed above, Twitter and Facebook pose other challenges. Scandals, big and small, have erupted from unfortunate Tweets and Facebook posts. Examples abound from every social media site. *Time* magazine created a top-ten list of Twitter scandals from 2011, which can be found online.[11]

Think about why you want to connect via social media. What do you hope to accomplish? Whom do you want to reach? And why? Are you merely homesick and wanting to reach out? Unless you absolutely must make a call or check a message, put your devices away. But keep your notebook handy, which we've encouraged all along. The notebook is simple and far less distracting than a Smartphone or iPad, with their time-consuming applications. New phone technology can be the handheld equivalent of cable television, where you can waste an afternoon clicking through hundreds of channels. So, using any number of the exercises we've done in other chapters—like writing about place, people, or language—make notes on interesting observations and things heard. Keep your notes factual. Later, maybe just before bed, polish a couple of Tweets or a Facebook post. Or don't. Maybe do some freewriting in your journal instead.

THE PLEASURES AND HAZARDS OF GPS AND OTHER DEVICES

In "Real Adventurers Read Maps," Steven Kurutz argues that we lose something essential when we give up paper maps to be guided by GPS or ask Siri to direct us. When we have to read signs and be alert to our surroundings, "That closer engagement . . . imprints the landscape more vividly and permanently."[12] With a companion traveler, we must work as a team when navigating with a map, one person offering directions, the other following. Above all, when immersed in technology, we lose the serendipity of surprise that unexpected byways and back roads offer. It's akin to what we sacrifice to purely digital libraries that offer no chance of happening on the unexpected book next to the one you were seeking. Like all new technologies, GPS has pros and cons. If you're pressed for time or need to stay on main routes for other reasons, a GPS may be perfect. But ponder the words of Eric Riback, author of the blog *Mapville*, who told Kurutz that a simple map's importance is in the "seeking, dreaming part of travel that you can do with a map."[13]

Fieldwork Exercise One

Choose a journey you can go on twice, perhaps within a day's drive. Go first by car with a GPS. Use your journal to record notes before, during (pulled over, of course), and after the journey. Repeat the trip and the exercise, using a paper map. You can reverse this order and/or add train or bus travel, each time comparing positives and negatives of paper versus technology. What is lost, what gained? Be attentive to details you miss or add with each trip.

RESEARCH ON THE GROUND

When you enter a new country, find out what people are doing with social media. Visit a mobile phone store. As you buy a smart card for use inside a cellular phone, talk to the proprietor about local phone and Internet culture. Do people use Internet cafés? In many parts of the world, Internet cafés were abundant ten years ago. But Wi-Fi access and cell phones now allow people to text and check e-mail and the Internet easily without a computer, making the cafés obsolete. But if you find one, hang out and use a computer, noting how others use the space and the technology, and what the costs are. Interview residents on how technology has changed their lives. In West Africa, for example, people pay for cell phone time with scratch cards they buy on the street. The cards have become a currency unto themselves. Take taxis and ask drivers how they communicate with each other and how they find fares. Take notes on your observations.

RESEARCH ON THE WORLD WIDE WEB

We now consult the Internet so often that it's difficult to remember that not all information sources are equally reliable. Since the Internet includes vast commercial, governmental, educational, and other networks, searching with a browser like Google or Yahoo! carries us into the brave if no longer so new world of the World Wide Web. The web is especially useful for a first hit of information. See what's out there and then begin sifting and evaluating.

For example, we looked at Wikipedia to brush up on basic terms for this chapter, such as the word "Internet" and the word "hypertext." But we also question what we find on Wikipedia, remembering that its open process of editing is both a strength and potential weakness. As you research online, remember that many websites have not been vetted by editors and other knowledgeable gatekeepers. Some have been peer reviewed by people with specific expertise, some have not. Also bear in mind that traditional gatekeepers can be wrong or can be influenced by the politics of academic or social worlds, nepotism, and other human factors. Whether doing traditional print research or searching the web, always remain critically alert. Look for information that both challenges and affirms your on-the-ground observations. Weigh where particular information comes from, who serves as editor, and keep track of all sources. Think critically as you research.

Let's say you were in Israel during the 2014 outbreak of violence with Hamas. You've done preliminary research on the creation of Israel as well as on the current situation of the Palestinian people. You've interviewed Arabs and Israelis to get first-person accounts of this complicated history and how people actually live with ongoing conflict. You turn to social media to keep abreast of daily events, views from around the world, and the perspectives of friends and family in the United States. But what you might find is what annoys many people: social media can create a bubble that reinforces existing attitudes rather than opening up discussion. Writing in the online magazine *Medium* in 2014, Gilad Lotan argues that "not only is there much more media produced, but it is coming at us at a faster pace, from many more sources. As we construct our online profiles based on what we already know, what we're interested in, and what we're recommended, social networks are perfectly designed to reinforce our existing beliefs."[14]

Sometimes just posting something online will connect you to others in unexpected ways that energize a project. Consider the story of John Maloof, the amateur historian and photographer who discovered the work of street photographer Vivian Maier. While writing a history of his Chicago neighborhood, he bought a box of her negatives at auction that he thought might provide needed photos for the book. None proved useful so he set it aside for several months. Later he posted about a hundred of her photos online, a site that generated little interest. Then, a little over a year later, he posted a discussion on Flickr to the group HCSP (Hardcore Street Photography). Responders overwhelmingly encouraged Maloof to create an archive. He promoted Maier's work all over the world and his efforts inspired him to make the probing documentary *Finding Vivian Maier*.[15] Without that online connection, none of this might have happened. So don't be afraid to use the Internet to connect but be discreet, thoughtful, ethical, and culturally sensitive.

A helpful research guide is Don MacLeod's 2012 book, *How to Find Out Anything: From Extreme Google Searches to Scouring Government Documents, a Guide to Uncovering Anything about Everyone and Everything*. MacLeod, a law librarian and legal researcher, writes that some of the best resources are the simplest. He recommends consulting reference librarians and expertly staffed and fact-checked websites like Britannica.com. They can save a lot of time, helping you to separate reliable facts from false information. "A good library catalog," he adds, "is a near perfect tool for finding experts."[16]

---✔---

Fieldwork Exercise Two

Here are some suggestions for advance research in the library and on the Internet. Before you arrive in a place, surf the web and establish who is Tweeting or posting material from the country where you're headed. Tap into national newspapers and broadcast media as well as local bloggers and Tweeters. Search websites, blogs, and government web pages for a list of continuously updated information you can access when you arrive. This includes weather and road conditions, embassy travel information, and sites specific to your journey.

In some places—particularly Africa, South America, Asia, and parts of Eastern Europe—you might find Peace Corps blogs to be helpful. Some are independent posts by volunteers, in addition to those on the Peace Corps blog site (https://www.peacecorps.gov/returned-volunteers/awards/blog-it-home/). You can also type in the name of the country you want to visit and the keywords "Peace Corps blogs." Tweets and blogs of other foreign travelers are useful as well. Find out what concerns local social media users in politics, arts and culture, and daily life. As you depart, take this list of online resources with you.

Early in 2012, just before Peter went to Mali to report on turmoil in that country, he had difficulty finding good information about what was happening in the capital, which had been rocked by a coup. Peter found one consistent blogger, a Fulbright scholar and former Mali Peace Corps volunteer named Bruce Whitehouse, who had stayed in Mali in defiance of a U.S. Embassy evacuation order. He also found a steady Tweet stream by an Associated Press stringer. While reading their reports, he established e-mail contact with both sources. They helped him understand what to expect on the ground when he flew in.

PERSONAL SECURITY

The online world is fraught with risks, from credit card use to self-revelation through social media. For thousands of years, travelers have been vulnerable to con artists and banditry. As you travel, it's not a good idea to reveal your location and itinerary online. The less people know about what you're doing and where you're going, the better, though this is more critical for some places (politically unstable countries, for instance) than others. It's harder to protect yourself in a foreign environment where you may not speak the language. You can access the Twitter website to change the settings so your Tweets don't reveal your location (https://support.twitter .com/articles/78525-faqs-about-the-tweet-location-feature).

The FBI has a sobering website on the risks of using social media, including while traveling (http://www.fbi.gov/about-us/investigate /counterintelligence/internet-social-networking-risks). Another excellent resource to check out before you go is Larry Habegger's *World Travel Watch* blog on the World Hum website (http://www .worldhum.com/features/world-travel-watch/), which offers the latest on what to look out for around the world.

LONG FORM SOCIAL MEDIA: THE BLOG

The blog offers a long form outlet for your travel writing, one that creates a new balance of power with traditional magazines and other outlets. The exposure for your work and the conversations you create with readers can be fun, engaging, and educational. But blogs raise practical and ethical questions. First, competition for readers is intense. WordPress.com, a popular software program for launching websites and blogs, reports there are seventy-four million WordPress.com sites alone. Nielsen, the company that follows global consumer and marketing trends, tracked 181 million blogs by the end of 2011. The best way to beat the competition is to write clearly and vividly, to research thoroughly, and to fact-check your work carefully.

It helps to have institutional support. As mentioned above, the Peace Corps promotes accurate, well-written blogs that meet the agency's mission. They select and promote the best work from a contest called "Blog It Home." Another Peace Corps website that features the best volunteer blogging is "Standing out Abroad Becomes Vital for Change" (https://www.peacecorps.gov/stories/how-standing -out-abroad-becomes-vital-for-change/). Students studying abroad often write blogs as well, including the digital stories and visual artwork discussed in chapter 4. One excellent resource is CAPA: The Global Education Network (http://capaworld.capa.org/10-study -abroad-travel-blogs-to-inspire-you).

As bloggers, we have to be our own fact-checkers and ethical ombudsmen. All social media developments have made it easy to just write and send without thinking. The consequences are bad writing, inaccurate reporting, and/or thoughtless and hurtful opinionating. In 2007, the software developer Tim O'Reilly published a "Bloggers Code of Conduct":

Take responsibility not just for your own words, but for the comments you allow on your blog.

Label your tolerance level for abusive comments.

Consider eliminating anonymous comments.

Don't feed the trolls.

Take the conversation offline, and talk directly, or find an intermediary who can do so. [We suggest you ignore abusive trolls.]

If you know someone who is behaving badly, tell them so.

Don't say anything online that you wouldn't say in person.[17]

This now reads like common sense. Many blogger codes have since added to and polished the tenets set out by O'Reilly.

PRACTICAL MATTERS

Setting up a blog is easy. Sites like www.blogspot.com and www .wordpress.com offer tutorials for obtaining a domain name, designing your blog site, and finding a server platform like www .godaddy.com or www.yahoo.com to host your blog. A simple Google survey will show you many more sites. You will have to pay an annual fee for the domain name and to the server.

The following exercise echoes what writers have done for ages to launch their careers and find venues for their work. Study the marketplace. You may find it more useful to contribute to someone else's blog, allowing others to judge your work before publication. This might be a good way to refine your work and learn more about the trade before setting up your own site.

Fieldwork Exercise Three

Research web magazines and blogs—the good, the bad, the awful. List sites that are well-researched and designed, well-written, and fun to read. These are your models. Also get a feel for those that are sloppy, poorly written, a chore to read, and even offensive. Avoid their mistakes.

Suggested Sites

There are many fine blogs and websites you can read for free. Some stick to travel while others cover travel with other subjects and genres, including fiction and poetry. For example the literary journal *Ascent* (www.readthebestwriting.com) prides itself on publishing new writers. It's well edited with a simple design but like many high-quality literary journals, it pays nothing. Other sites, like World Hum (www.worldhum.com), offer payment and host excellent blogs on issues like travel security and health. World Hum is one of the best free travel writing sites you can find. We have already mentioned a few good blogs, and here are a few more:

> *Accidental Theologist: An Agnostic Eye on Religion, Politics, and Existence* (www.accidentaltheologist.com)
> *Atavist Magazine* (https://magazine.atavist.com/)
> *Brevity: A Journal of Concise Literary Nonfiction* (www.brevity.com)
> *Defunct: A Literary Repository for the Ages* (www.defunctmag.com)
> *Guernica: A Magazine of Global Arts and Politics* (www.guernicamag.com)
> *Huffington Post* (www.huffingtonpost.com)
> *Nowhere* magazine (www.nowheremag.com)
> *New York Times's Borderlines* blog (http://opinionator.blogs.nytimes.com/category/borderlines/)
> *Salon* (www.salon.com)
> *Terrain.org: A Journal of the Built + Natural Environments* (www.terrain.org)

Smart Set (www.thesmartset.com)

Vagabonding: The Uncommon Guide to the Art of Long-Term World Travel (www.vagabonding.net)

Vela: Written by Women (www.velamag.com)

CRAFT DISCUSSION: ARE BLOGS LITERARY?

Certainly they are. Major media outlets like the *Atlantic Monthly* and the *New Yorker* feature fine literary blogs, as do journals like *Terrain.org*, *Nowhere* magazine, and the rest of those listed above, as well as many others. But some people blog badly. They launch ideas and opinions without thoughtful review, fact-checking, or a feel for how to write in clear, concise language. No one will read work written without a sense of audience. "You can't just start writing and expect to gain readers with no effort," writes Diane Nadin, writing coach at the Writers Bureau (www.writersbureau.com), a website based in the United Kingdom. "You will have to spend time thinking up topics, writing interesting posts and publishing them. What you consider interesting may not be so great for your readers."[18]

One way to circumvent your own blinders is to include the perspectives of people from the culture you're exploring. Say you want to write about the gradual disappearance of rickshaw drivers in India. Maybe you view this as a tragic loss of a distinct culture. Some people may agree, while others welcome modern transport. In either case, you increase your audience by widening your point of view.

Writing Exercise Three

Begin a blog entry with writing for twenty minutes. Choose a subject you think will have wide appeal. At a magazine, you'd have to "pitch" that idea to editors, so try pitching your idea to friends. Give yourself a thousand words. Then interview someone on that subject and include his or her opinion in the blog.

The same caveats for Facebook and Twitter apply to blogs. As journalist and blogger Luke O'Neill wrote in a December 2013 essay in *Esquire*: "The Internet . . . is a ravenous beast that eats alive anyone who can't answer its hoary riddle," that riddle being the Internet's vast tangle of hoaxes, inaccuracies, and just plain bad writing.[19]

Beyond regret lie greater risks. Employers—Google, for example—have fired employees for blogging critically about the company. If you're going to publish, you have to be open to critique. If you confuse facts or attract the attention of authorities and others in a foreign country, and are writing critically, you might anger people. Bloggers face the same risks and criticism journalists do. Adam Nossiter, who covered West Africa for the *New York Times,* has been threatened with arrest many times. Andrew Sullivan, a committed blogger who has written several books and once served as editor of the *New Republic,* celebrates the risks of blogging. On his blog, the *Dish*, Sullivan wrote in February 2015 that blogging "means writing dangerously with the only assurance—without an editor— that readers will correct you when you're wrong and encourage you when you are right. It is a terrifying and exhilarating way to write— and also an emotionally, psychologically depleting one."[20]

Keep in mind as well the longevity of writing on the web. It's nearly impossible to delete information once it's been grabbed by the huge search mechanisms of Google and Yahoo. Individuals with high public profiles can employ services to "clean" unwanted Internet material. They can bury negative content so it's harder to find but they can't delete it.

A case in point: one student on an overseas program posted a story critical of her host brother on her personal blog. When asked to reconsider, she refused. She wasn't an insensitive person; she was angry and wanted to vent. But she couldn't comprehend the longevity or potential reach of her blog. Would he ever read it? Perhaps, perhaps not, but the writing will have a long life on the Internet. You can't know the lengths your words might travel or how your attitudes might change, rendering your current feelings a future embarrassment. This isn't to say you can't write negative reviews of people or places. But you need to attend to the nuances of good writing and the ethical responsibilities of the traveler. Had this student worked with a writing group, she might have learned to reveal multiple points of view, to consider the cultural differences between her and her host brother, and to fine-tune the writing to tap the complexity of human encounters. She also might have hidden her host brother's identity. Our writing should enhance, not obstruct, cross-cultural understanding.

Writing Exercise Four

Here's an exercise for the aspiring blogger and a chance to adapt some exercises cited in previous chapters. Describe a difficult situation, one you didn't understand or where you were angry or frustrated. Tell the story rapidly, beginning with "The way I see it . . ." Get out all that emotion. Then write again in the third person from the other person's point of view, beginning with "Perhaps he [or she] sees it . . ." After both segments, do a freewrite beginning with "Looking back at this situation . . ."

Good writing demands discipline. Develop a critical distance from your work and recruit a strong circle of readers you trust to ask tough questions before you post anything to your blog. Use the guidelines suggested in chapter 9 for how to form a response group. Your writing will improve with your blog.

Finally, think about the timing of your posts. Can they wait until your travels are over or can you post them outside the chronology of your travels? Some writing needs to gestate so we can ponder the meaning of the experience.

REVISION

With your Tweets, blog posts, or other writing, revision is critical. If you want to send work to literary magazines or journals, bear in mind that blogs are usually considered published material. Therefore, a blog post may not be accepted as unpublished unless it's substantially revised. Always be up-front about the status of work that's been on your blog.

Revision Exercise One

Go back to your list of Tweets. Using each one as the beginning of a paragraph, create an essay that tells a story in fragments, following the model of Teju Cole's Tweets described above. Make each one less than a page. Identify each by asterisks or list with Roman numerals.

Remember our discussion of Tom Wolfe and status detail in chapter 5? Another good exercise would be to whittle down your status detail observations into Tweets. Or use that fifty-nine character African proverb that caught your ear: "When your neighbor's house is burning, you better take care." Or something you saw once in northern Africa: "Small boy riding huge double humped camel down sandy street" (eighty-three characters). Or: "Parking Paris style: Seen on the Champs Elysees: 2 men lift compact Renault from street into tight parking space" (113 characters).

Revision Exercise Two

Send a draft of a blog post to friends. Ask them to respond using the simple guidelines outlined in chapter 9. Revise before you post the story.

Social media offers enormous opportunity for travelers, students of culture, and people dealing with civil crises or natural disasters to share what they witness and learn. But hone your skills in discernment and restraint as you write.

After Hurricane Sandy, a 2012 Pew Research report stated that Twitter "was a critical lifeline throughout the disaster."[21] But social media was also responsible for significant misinformation, including the erroneous Twitter report that the Con Edison company was shutting off power to Manhattan. That started from a single Tweet that snowballed, frightening many people and causing some to put themselves at higher risk by fleeing their homes unnecessarily.

When you travel, stay focused. Be prudent about using social media. It might be helpful to consider these lines from T. S. Eliot's poem "Burnt Norton":

Filled with fancies and empty of meaning
Tumid apathy with no concentration
Men and bits of paper, whirled by the cold wind
That blows before and after.[22]

2

—

RETURN AND REVISION

9

REVISING YOUR WRITING

AND YOUR LIFE

You've been gone for a month or five years. Your passport is worn from passing through so many hands. You've realized Graham Greene's prediction that life will never be "quite the same" after crossing a border. Your notebooks brim with stories half written, begging expansion. As you revise your writing, you may also discover changes in your sense of self.

John Irving once said that half of his life was an act of revision—a reference to the ambiguous terrain between art and life. Our revised selves emerge from the writing as well as from the journey itself. Cynthia Ozick, who contrasted the traveler passing through a place with a place passing through the traveler, added to that opposition: "A visitor comes either to teach or to learn, or perhaps simply and neutrally to observe; but a pilgrim comes on purpose to be taught renewal."[1] The hard work of revision can offer a glimpse of a renewed life.

Consider an historical example of the commitment to revision. In 1919, less than a year after the end of World War I, a British army officer arrived by train at England's Reading Station. Somewhere in the confusion of changing trains, he left behind a briefcase, perhaps on the first train or in the station café. No one actually knows, and the officer could not remember. The luggage and the manuscript it contained have never been found, despite the fact that the officer, Lieutenant Colonel Thomas Edward Lawrence, who had recently returned from service in the Middle East, placed notices in newspapers all over Britain. Inside was the first draft, some two hundred thousand words of a memoir that would later be titled *The Seven Pillars of Wisdom*. The book detailed Lawrence's experience leading the Arab revolt against the Ottoman Turkish Empire during World War I in what is now Iraq, Syria, Kuwait, and Jordan. When he lost the briefcase, Lawrence had been shuttling back and forth between his home in England and Versailles, France, where the victors were negotiating the spoils of war and where his regional expertise was needed. Some of Lawrence's friends claimed the manuscript had been stolen for political reasons, though he insisted he lost it.

Lawrence set about rewriting the book from scratch. The second draft, which took more than two years to complete, was almost twice as long. When he created a third draft, Lawrence burned the second. A limited edition of that third, long version appeared in 1922, but Lawrence then cut the draft in half and published the more widely known version in 1926.

All of that work for one book! *The Seven Pillars of Wisdom* has been called memoir, travel writing, pure fiction, the ranting of a demented mind, and a fine example of the personal essay. Few books in English literature have been as highly praised and intensely damned. Winston Churchill called it "one of the greatest books ever written in the English language," while the late critic Christopher Hitchens dismissed the work, preferring to write of Lawrence himself as "the man who betrayed the Arabs" and died a "twisted and cynical recluse."[2] Most writers crave that kind of attention, positive or negative, from such highly placed pundits. Still, an enduring question some critics ask is whether the loss of the first draft improved or hurt Lawrence's process of revision and the final work. Even if the lost draft is found, the writer is gone and we will never know the answer. Yet the question still compels. After losing the briefcase, Lawrence reportedly began rewriting immediately, with the original draft and his memory of the desert war still fresh in his mind. From this and many other well-known episodes of authors and their lost manuscripts (Sylvia Plath, Maxine Hong Kingston, Toni Morrison, and V. S. Naipaul, to name a few) comes another practical lesson: save and back up your drafts.

The Seven Pillars of Wisdom, covering only two years in a man's life, took many more years to write through draft after draft after draft. Many accomplished writers can appreciate Lawrence's need to revise. Jack Kerouac revised compulsively. Hemingway famously said he rewrote the last page of *A Farewell to Arms* thirty-nine times. Decades ago, the novelist Elmore Leonard told *Newsweek*: "If it sounds like writing, I rewrite it."[3] Celebrated essayist Susan Sontag wrote: "I don't write easily or rapidly. My first draft usually has only a few elements worth keeping. I have to find what those are and build from them and throw out what doesn't work, or what simply is not alive."[4] Dorothy Parker—critic, poet, novelist, and screenwriter—told the *Paris Review* in 1956: "It takes me six months to do a story. . . . I can't write five words but that I can change seven."[5] *New Yorker* editor David Remnick said, "Revision is all there is."[6]

Many of us who teach writing know what it means to face our students with the reality of revision and have them look back at us stricken. Revision is hard. Revision can be tedious. But the process is always necessary and sometimes it can be compulsive fun. That pesky inner critic we urged you to banish in chapter 1 is now welcome. For just as we need to ignore the critic to generate first drafts, we need his or her discerning eye to push through multiple revisions.

For more evidence of the role of revision, look at the many people writers thank in the acknowledgments of their books:

teachers, editors, friends, agents, wives, husbands, lovers, and writing groups. For *The Spirit Catches You and You Fall Down*, Anne Fadiman thanks the entire Hmong community of Merced, California, who "were willing to share their sophisticated culture with me and who earned my passionate respect."[7] Ted Conover, journalist and travel writer, wrote in his acknowledgments to *Whiteout: Lost in Aspen* that his book had many "midwives" who helped shape the book.[8] For reading the manuscript of his classic book on the meaning of art, *The Gift*, Lewis Hyde thanks a friend who "managed to combine a stranger's cold eye with a sister's unconditional support."[9] May we all find a reader with that combination of talents!

You write alone but you revise with the help of your "midwives." Most good writing goes through many drafts. Each represents a progression, a sharpening, a smoothing out that moves closer to strong prose. There are writers—perhaps Paul Theroux is an example—who write a first draft, polish a bit, then publish, but they are rare.

DEVELOPMENT, EXPANSION, AND REVISION

Each chapter of this book offers a few revision exercises, but up until now, we've focused on drafting—that generative process of simply getting our words down. Writer Jim Heynen says producing first drafts should feel as free as singing in the shower. John Cage once told painter Philip Guston, "When you start working, everybody is in your studio—the past, your friends, enemies, the art world, and above all, your own ideas—all are there. But as you continue painting, they start leaving, one by one, and you are left completely alone. Then, if you're lucky, even you leave."[10] The writing process can free us from our conscious selves, including that inner critic.

That conscious self must return to revise. Some argue that the development process of adding material to flesh out a draft is part of revision, that "re-seeing" begins as soon as a freewrite ends. Regardless of where you think revision begins, it involves review, expansion, and clarification. These are not necessarily sequential but, rather, interwoven processes. When you expand a first freewrite, you don't just "add to and polish." In *Deep Revision*, Meredith Sue Willis says that this tinkering approach risks "merely hovering over the surface of your material. When I think of going deeper, I always think of mining: you tunnel in, dig out the ore, and eventually smelt it to separate out the metal."[11]

✔

Revision Exercise One—Development

Pat Schneider of the Amherst Writing Workshop suggests a focus on what feels most alive in our writing. With that in mind, find a freewrite from an assignment in a previous chapter, one you haven't yet revised much or at all. Review what you've written, preferably at one sitting. Underline phrases that intrigue you. Develop three new freewrites beginning each with one of those phrases. When you've accumulated enough material, put the pieces together, then review to see what's most compelling. You can continue this looping process for as long as you need to develop a working draft.

LEVELS OF REVISION

It's tempting to show your work to the midwives early on. Sometimes that works well, particularly in a class or a group of trusted listeners. But the wrong feedback too soon or from the wrong people can damage your work, dampening the search for your subject. Another temptation is to begin with copy editing, polishing those first sentences to make them sing. Resist that impulse as well. This isn't to say that you don't tinker as you write, changing a word or sentence here or there, adding bits as they occur to you. As Susan Bell states in *The Artful Edit*, "Most of us edit as we write and write as we edit . . . you edit a sentence and a new idea suddenly spins out from a word change, so you write a new paragraph where until that moment nothing else was needed. This is the ongoing edit."[12] Bell separates this process from the draft edit, where you stop and assess what you have. This is where levels of revision become critical.

Though it's hard to tease these apart, we revise best working from macro to micro levels. Macro—which includes meaning, structure, and other "big" issues—doesn't mean more important. The micro level of attention to sentences, paragraphs, and word choice can make or break a piece of writing. Both are fundamental.

MACRO REVISION: FINDING THE SUBJECT

You've finished a draft, celebrated that achievement, and let it rest for a while. It's time to take on the Big Issue of Meaning. Annie Dillard says, "When you write, you lay out a line of words. The line of words is a miner's pick, a woodcarver's gouge, a surgeon's probe. You wield it, and it digs a path you follow. Soon you find yourself in new territory. Is it a dead end, or have you located the real subject? You will know tomorrow or this time next year."[13]

What is your piece about? Sometimes the subject is hiding at the center, the ore waiting to be smelted. Sometimes it's in the first paragraph, other times hovering at the end. Meaning can be explicit or lurking under what is suggested. Donald Murray argues that revision is "a search for the central tension, the knot."[14] Some pieces have more than one overarching idea. Perhaps what seems to be the subject—your obsession with photographing clotheslines as you travel—is really about artistry in daily life and your revolt against art elitism in the United States. Vivian Gornick calls the context and perhaps the content of the piece "the situation," while the "story is the emotional experience that preoccupies the writer: the insight, the wisdom, the thing one has come to say."[15] What's crucial is to read first for meaning to discover what it is you have come to say.

Structure

You may have a structure in mind, perhaps one required for a magazine or academic assignment. We'll examine a number of literary forms in chapter 10. But even before facing a final decision about form, read your piece with an open mind about its design. A structure may be hovering under the surface, waiting to emerge. Does the narrative proceed chronologically or the inverse? Contrast a biography that moves from cradle to grave with one that opens with a deathbed scene. How do flashbacks serve the latter structure? Is it a classic narrative arc, with the story building to a climax, then descending toward its conclusion (discussed in chapter 10 under "memoir" forms)? If it's a linear essay, where does the main idea appear? If it feels fragmented, should it become a mosaic or lyric essay?

If you sense an emerging form, examine the mix of scene and summary. Which parts show through scenes and which give backstory through summary? Is the combination right or do you need to add dialogue to scenes, or more exposition to guide the reader? This scrutiny also helps at the micro level. But looking at scene and summary often makes sense in conjunction with macro-level revision.

As an experiment, cut your writing into segments. Move them into different combinations on the computer, or if you favor tactile sensations, onto a large piece of butcher-block paper. Disrupt the form to re-vision the writing. If it's prose, turn it into a poem or vice versa. Print it out in a new font. Change your reading environment—from home to a coffee shop or park bench. What are the options for this piece?

Audience

Writing for a particular publication or audience may dictate your revision process. But to plumb the heart of your experience abroad, banish thoughts of audience for first drafts. Get your ideas and stories onto the page. As soon as you begin to revise, let your audience back in. Are they friends and family at home reading your blog? An editor or professor who gave a specific assignment? Does your audience know a lot about your topic or nothing at all? In other words, what needs to be explained? As you read the draft, make notes in the margins.

Point of View, Voice, and Mood

Who tells the story? This is the point of view, even if you incorporate other people's words or include alternative perspectives. In fact, the addition of other voices might enhance writing about other cultures. Even if you alternate between first, second, and third person, the dominant point of view should be clear to a reader. Voice, as we discussed along with point of view in chapter 3, also means your style, distinctive quirks, ways of using language, and the attitude or personality established on the page.

Mood affects how a reader understands your work. If you're writing about attending a funeral overseas, the piece should re-create the mood. We might assume solemnity at a funeral, but that's not always the case. Details of the scene can dictate mood: how people dressed, their facial expressions, the smell of incense, perhaps, or the stories recited about the deceased.

Revision Exercise Two—Macro Level

1. Meaning: Go through and write in the margins of each section of a piece what that part is about or what it evokes for you. Is there a central theme or feeling, what Peter Elbow calls a center of gravity?

2. Structure: Using markers in different colors, mark passages as scenes or summarizing sections of the text. Do you rely more on one or the other?

3. Point of view and voice: Are the voice and tone appropriate for the content? Are you satisfied with the choice of first, second, or third person? Try telling the story from someone else's perspective, say, a participant in a wedding or a fruit seller in a market. Be sure, as we've indicated in other chapters, to frame your writing so the reader knows you're imagining another point of view.

MICRO REVISION: LANGUAGE

Zoë Heller, writing for the *New York Times Book Review* on whether writing can be taught, describes her daughter's surprise that eliminating the words "extremely," "totally," and "incredibly" from her writing strengthened her prose. "No one at my daughter's school has ever mentioned to her that the use of the word 'incredibly' is subject to the law of diminishing returns."[16] Not only can writing be taught, but we can also train ourselves to pay careful attention to language and banish habits that weaken our work.

Question qualifiers

Sometimes our habits as writers emerge most prominently as we revise. These include overuse of adjectives and adverbs. Mark Twain said, "As to the adjective: when in doubt, strike it out."[17] As parts of language, these obviously serve a function, but we do best to hold them in reserve. When an adjective is needed, weigh overused words ("good," "just," "small") against more descriptive ones ("fine," "barely," "minute"). Appraise the context for an adjective that amplifies a noun. You can also substitute a descriptive noun. A woman's "pallor" tells us more than her "pale skin." Nouns that capture nuances of language show us what the writer sees.

Strong verbs can replace weak adverb-verb combinations. We often rely on adverbs, especially those ending in "ly" to describe how an action is performed. "She carefully picked up the pencil" is vague; the reader does not know what "carefully" means in terms of actual physical movement. Details illustrate action better than adverbs: "She picked up the pencil by cradling the eraser between her thumb and index finger." Specifics will energize your work. You can also substitute a verb. "Strode" shows us someone who walked quickly.

A caveat: we can deaden our creativity if we observe these exercises too zealously (see? there's an adverb). Weigh each choice as you revise with your own voice and goals in mind.

Question Use of the Verb "to Be"

"To be"—"I am," "she is," etc.—is a workhorse verb of the English language needed for many constructions. But we may wear out this helpmate. Writing teachers often ask students to write a paragraph without the verb "to be" in any form. This exercise forces the writer to closely consider how active verbs energize a sentence. Disciplining yourself to use more active verbs will enliven your writing toward a more vivid style.

Passive Voice: Problems and Misconceptions

Passive voice has a gotten a bum rap, sometimes deservedly. "Mistakes were made by the director" renders the actor impotent, while "the director made mistakes" clarifies the action and responsibility. The first example also illuminates how passive voice might serve political ends. But passive voice has a place. Linguist Steven Pinker writes, "Linguistic research has shown that the passive construction has a number of indispensable functions because of the way it engages a reader's attention and memory. A skilled writer should know what those functions are and push back against copy editors who, under the influence of grammatically naïve style guides, blue-pencil every passive construction they spot into an active one."[18]

Another potential pitfall is jargon. Specific disciplines or occupations may require specialized language, but it rarely appeals to a general audience. Tom Wolfe's famous comment about the "beige voice" or "beige tone" of certain kinds of writing is a useful reminder here.[19] Even if writing for an institution, say the Peace Corps or a university or a specialized publication, you can strive for clarity, clear language, and compelling prose.

Avoid Redundancy and Run-on Sentences

The novelist and critic Francine Prose accentuated the need for revision in a 2011 interview: "It's useful to develop a kind of terror of boring the reader," she said. "Because the reader isn't endlessly patient like your friends or teachers."[20] A good way to bore the reader is repetition without intention.

Often, particularly in early drafts, we restate words, phrases, or ideas. This happens as we work out what we want to say. Sometimes we turn caretaker, certain that if we say it one more time our readers won't miss our meaning. But readers need space for their own interpretations. The unsaid is as essential as what's stated.

Reading aloud helps catch "tics" such as repetition that get under a reader's skin. Another is the run-on sentence. If you have to catch your breath reading, the sentence may be too long. But not all extended sentences qualify as run-ons. Proper punctuation, musical prose, and clear relationships between clauses can make a long sentence sing. Consider the opening of Charles Dickens's *A Tale of Two Cities*:

It was the best of times, it was the worst of times, it was the age of wisdom, it was the age of foolishness, it was the epoch of belief, it was the epoch of incredulity, it was the season of Light, it was the season of Darkness, it was the spring of hope, it was the winter of despair, we had everything before us, we had nothing before us, we were all going direct to Heaven, we were all going direct the other way—in short, the period was so far like the present period, that some of its noisiest authorities insisted on its being received, for good or for evil, in the superlative degree of comparison only.[21]

It's hard to argue that Dickens should have sliced up such a magnificent sentence. The Portuguese novelist José Saramago created a distinct style of page-long sentences with sparing use of periods or even commas. But a reader of Dickens or Saramago recognizes these as stylistic choices; otherwise they would seem annoying.

Longer sentences also generate rhythm, a quality as necessary to prose as to poetry. Try alternating sentence length, following expansive phrases with short, staccato ones. If your natural bent is longer sentences, make them clear. Editor Susan Bell argues that "baroque prose demands tremendous rigor."[22]

Good readers in a workshop or writing group can identify our tics as we expand and revise our writing.

Revision Exercise Three—Micro Level

1. Go through one of your essays and identify all the adverbs and adjectives. Try replacing adverb-verb combinations such as "recommended strongly" with verbs like "urged" or adjective-noun combinations with nouns, for example, "tot" instead of "small boy."

2. Choose a freewrite and replace as many "to be" forms as you can with other verbs. Aim for 70 percent. Then change all the passive verb forms to active ones. Reread to ensure you haven't eliminated passive voice when it was in fact the right choice.

3. Read a draft aloud to yourself or a partner. Focus on repetition, redundancies, and other problems. The places where you stumble—a sentence with too many prepositional phrases, a glitch in syntax, a statement that is vague or doesn't make sense—signal the need for revision. Make a list of your own habits and create some exercises to weed out the tics you want to eliminate.

This is not an exhaustive list or discussion of ways to revise at the micro level. You'll find what works best in your individual process as you assess your work. Style guides are indispensable. Here are several good ones:

The Associated Press Stylebook is necessary for every creative nonfiction writer who hopes to publish in magazines.

The Elements of Style, by William Strunk and E. B. White, is a classic brief guide to style.

A useful online guide is Paul Brians's site Common Errors in English Usage (http://public.wsu.edu/~brians/errors/). Brians is a retired English professor (Washington State University).

Grammar Girl is another valuable website (http://www.quickanddirtytips
.com/education/grammar).

Drafts left by other writers are great teachers. A learning opportunity disappeared when T. E. Lawrence lost the first draft of *The
Seven Pillars of Wisdom* and burned the second. We will never know
for sure if the revised manuscripts improved on the earlier ones. But
we can read other examples from writers like Hemingway, who was
a ruthless editor. He left behind manuscripts heavily annotated with
his edits. Hemingway—to borrow a phrase from the Cornish novelist
Arthur Quiller-Couch—knew how to "murder [his] darlings."[23]

The film *A River Runs through It*, based on the memoir by writer
and Shakespeare scholar Norman Maclean, features a compelling
example of revision. Maclean's father, a Methodist minister, home-
schooled his two sons and instilled meticulous writing habits. "My
father believed that the art of writing lay in thrift," states the film's
narrator. One scene shows Maclean's father returning an essay assignment with the curt instruction, "Half as long." When young
Maclean gives him the revised version, his father reads and hands it
back. "Again," he says, "half as long."[24]

Stephen Koch calls this kind of editing the "Ten Percent Solution."[25] Maybe you can't cut your piece in half, but slicing off that
10 percent you thought essential will lift and tighten your prose. We
need this kind of discipline. The cliché that we all love the sound
of our own voice may not be literally true of the spoken word but
it often applies to written work.

To summarize, here are some suggestions for editing your own
work drawn from this and other chapters. You can print this out
and keep it by your computer or mix and match these elements to
best suit your expansion, revision, and editing process.

1. Develop the practice of review, expansion, and clarification. These
   are not necessarily sequential but interwoven.
   A. Print a hardcopy of your drafts. You may be able to revise on the
      computer, but most people work differently with hard copy and

physical handling of the work. Try both methods to see what
works best.

B. Review what you've written silently, preferably at one sitting, to
find connections and coherence. Then read the piece aloud.

C. Expand internally—Go back and underline phrases and ideas
that intrigue you. Freewrite to expand the story, to discover new
ideas, images, and uses of language.

D. Expand externally—Mark the lines/segments that seem not to
belong, that feel like digressions. Freewrite on those lines, pushing to the edges of your piece.

2. Revision—Begin with the macro level, then move to the micro as we
described in this chapter.

A. Macro level: revise for meaning, structure, audience, mood, voice,
and point of view

B. Micro level: question qualifiers, use of the verb "to be," passive
voice, redundancy, run-on sentences, and other tics.

C. On a final edit, read aloud again. Ruthlessly delete unnecessary
words.

Finally, remember that guidelines are useful tools not mandates.
All are open to revision.

CRAFT DISCUSSION: THE WORKSHOP MODEL
AND RESPONDING TO WRITING

All along we've suggested that response from others is essential to
the writing process. Before sending out final work, getting feedback from trusted readers can save us from delivering half-baked
ideas or sloppy prose. Often a gap exists between what's in our
minds and what we get down on the page. In *Madame Bovary*, Flaubert captures the dilemma in his description of where language fails
us: "None of us can ever express the exact measure of our needs, or
our ideas, or our sorrows, and human speech is like a cracked kettle
on which we beat our tunes for bears to dance to, when we long
to inspire pity in the stars."[26] That chasm may seem unbridgeable

as we strain to see what's missing, what could be cut, and what's worth keeping. But readers and listeners can identify those lacunae and help mend the crack in the kettle.

Learning to offer helpful responses requires training and discipline. It's critical to find readers you can trust, people who understand and respect what you are doing, but who can challenge you as well. With some exceptions, spouses and relatives are not the best choices.

Many writers don't know how to ask for or receive critical response. A number of writing books include valuable guidelines. Peter Elbow's *Writing without Teachers* is an excellent example. Judith Barrington's *Writing the Memoir: From Truth to Art* includes a chapter on response groups, as do many other writing books. The websites of Colorado State University and numerous other universities feature information on how to form a writing group that meets face-to-face or online as well as ways to give and receive feedback.[27]

If you are a blogger, resist that temptation to post writing without trusted editors (friends or others) having read and critiqued the work. You can also submit writing to a blogging contest. The Peace Corps, for example, runs such a contest to promote high-quality blogs among its techno-savvy, social media–minded volunteers. We covered this in chapter 8, but for good measure the contest is called Blog It Home.[28]

Here are some preliminary guidelines for ways of responding to someone else's writing:

- Begin with something positive. Focus on a strong aspect of the work—the kernel of a great idea, a well-wrought phrase, the beginnings of a good organizational structure, or a thorough understanding of the material.
- Do not impose your own style on someone else's work, as in: "That's not how I would write it" or "This is how you should . . ." Try to understand the writer's goals. Do close reading or listening and ask questions.

- Imagine yourself on the receiving end of the comment. If this were your work, what would be helpful?
- Respond to the writing, not the writer. Instead of saying, "You should have started it this way," say, "This beginning stopped me ..." Some groups insist that responders refer to the writer as the "narrator" to differentiate the living person from the character on the page.
- Speak from your own perspective, describing your response as you read or listened, "I had to reread this section ..." Acknowledge that there may be a variety of opinions about the piece of writing.
- To reiterate our discussion above, start with the big issues: What is the piece about? What is its structure? Then move on to specifics by using the following tools adapted from Peter Elbow's "Ways of Responding":
  » Pointing/noticing. Point to language that is striking or powerful. You don't need to explain why.
  » Summary and sayback. Repeat back to the writer or summarize what you've heard or read.
  » Central point/ center of gravity. If this is a formal essay, can you state the main idea in one sentence? Or is the center of gravity a feeling?
  » Readers' or listeners' questions. Tell the writer what you want to know more about.
  » What's lurking. Is there something under the surface that is struggling to be said?
  » Points of confusion. Is there a place where you stumbled or had to reread?[29]

Receiving response gracefully also requires practice. Many groups ask that the writer remain silent and simply write down the responders' comments to ponder later. If you're working online, this won't be relevant, but other issues addressed below will be.

- Remember that your responders are trying to aid your writing process. Accept the gift of their time and thoughts.
- Realize that everyone hears or reads differently. What one reader finds confusing another might find crystal clear. But if five people out of six find something difficult to understand, consider revision.

- Learn to balance the opinions of others with your own goals. Peter Elbow says: "The reader is always right; the writer is always right." Keep this paradox in mind.
- Listen to praise with the same intensity that you listen to criticism. We often obsess over the one negative comment in a sea of positive ones.
- Use your listeners' or readers' feedback as a way to chart your own patterns, growth, and development as a writer.

William Blake wrote, "Without contraries, there is no progression." Debbie Lee, a critic and scholar of Blake studies, echoes his call. An artist who does not welcome critique or challenges, Lee argues, will not grow as an artist. "Without contraries we fall into cliché," she writes. "We think conventionally, and we rest in complacency."[30] Improvement of your work comes through confrontation with those contraries, with yourself, and with the writing.

T. E. Lawrence lived a life in conflict on many levels—within his family and through his adventures and misadventures, in war and diplomacy. But his main dispute was with himself, as his writings show and his biographers seem to agree. His diligent and exhaustive revision of *The Seven Pillars of Wisdom* reveals how exacting he was. Yet critics now view the end result as less polished than Lawrence hoped. "In truth," writes biographer Scott Anderson, "*Seven Pillars* is a fabulously uneven book, its occasional soaring lyricism and startling psychological insights all too often subsumed by long disquisitions on topography and a riot of local place names and fleeting characters likely to leave the reader struggling."[31]

Maybe Lawrence was aware of this. The loss of the original draft pained him for the rest of his life. In 1930, he complained in a letter to a friend that the lost draft was "shorter, snappier, and more truthful than the present version."

Shorter and snappier. Maybe.

We can only hope that Lawrence's original manuscript is still out there, gathering dust or molding in the humid English summer in some attic or basement, waiting to be discovered.

THE VARIETIES OF

LITERARY FORM

In 2010, Patti Smith, the singer-songwriter, poet, and sometime cultural provocateur, published a memoir, *Just Kids*, about her early relationship with the late artist and photographer Robert Mapplethorpe. The book won the National Book Award in nonfiction, surprising many fans who identified Smith, the so-called Godmother of Punk, with underground music and poetry, not prose. In fact, Smith has continually reinvented herself through different forms of artistic and political expression, including painting, photography, and music. Her entire career rests on pushing literary and other boundaries. In performance, she has sometimes dressed in men's clothes, including shirt and tie, to confront rock music's male domination. Her lauds include induction into the Rock and Roll Hall of Fame and the French Ministry of Culture's recognition as a Commander of the Ordre des Arts et des Lettres. She reviews both poetry and prose for the *New York Times Book Review* and other venues. When it comes to form, Patti Smith is all about variety.

Talented as she is, Smith is also an advocate of hard work. In *Just Kids*, she described Mapplethorpe's work ethic in perfecting his photography and how his "ability to concentrate for long periods infected me."[1] Smith learned from the hours Mapplethorpe spent studying Michelangelo's famous sculpture, *Slaves*, "wishing to access the feeling of working with the human form without the labor of the hammer and chisel."[2]

As a musician, artist, and writer, Smith studied the rules, then learned to break them with real impact. As we approach literary form, we would do well to emulate Smith and Mapplethorpe's model of hard work, discovery of the rules, and eventually, experimentation. To understand the work of writers you admire, begin with examining their literary forms.

Writing Exercise One

Make a list of nonfiction works that have been important to you—full-length books or shorter forms like essays. Choose one to write about in depth, freewriting on where and when you read the work. Why did it have an impact on you? Reread first for pleasure and meaning, then a second time to dissect the structure. What are the sections and subsections? The mix of scenes and backstory? You might return to the self-editing section of chapter 8 and use the same tools to analyze someone else's writing. Write in the margins or outline parts with highlighters to clarify form.

CREATIVE NONFICTION FORMS

As we discussed in the last chapter, sometimes we uncover a form lurking in our writing; other times we impose one structure after another onto the material until we get it right. Creating form, part serendipity, part craft, evolves during revision. Remember that to "re-see" considers content and form. Some nonfiction is characterized as much by length as theme. "Long form" is usually more than twenty-five thousand words (about a hundred pages), which might mean you're shaping a book.

Some writers use building metaphors to talk about formal variation. In *Writing Life Stories*, Bill Roorbach describes academic writing as "a row of identical townhouses in Anytown, U.S.A—nice, solid-brick construction . . ." Formal journalism is "Levittown, Long Island . . .—liveable, serviceable, functional, three models to choose from," while creative nonfiction includes back-to-the-land hippie cabins, geodesic domes, yurts, tree houses, and a host of others.[3] As we build structures, we may draw from others' architectural designs, cut up the plans, mix elements of a staid townhouse in Georgetown with a Quonset hut in an Alaskan village. Creative nonfiction welcomes innovation as long as you build a staircase for the reader to enter and experience the interior of your structure.

Roorbach's description seems more apt each year, as the field of creative nonfiction continues to expand. Among the myriad possibilities for nonfiction are essay, memoir, and others included in this chapter. Any of these might overlap with or come under the umbrella of "travel writing." Below are some categories and varied approaches to try. Feel free to mix and match strategies, changing freewrite prompts to suit your journey toward final form.

Travel Writing

Throughout the book, we've noted examples from the vast array of styles and forms that travel writing—past and present—encompasses. As Peter Whitfield notes, "The travel genre is so difficult to define because it is so inclusive—anything can get into it."[4] Though we've focused this book on nonfiction, travelogues have taken shape as fiction, poetry, and drama. Varied plots have and continue to animate the journey: the search for home; the rebirth of the self via the other; the quest for a lost object, family member, or ancestral story; the spiritual pilgrimage, just to name a few. The journey theme animates classic works such as the biblical *Book of Exodus*, Homer's *Odyssey*, and the Mesopotamian *Gilgamesh Epic*. The fifth-century Greek historian Herodotus, cited in chapter 1, recounted travel tales that continue to inspire writers such as Michael Ondaatje. The hero of his celebrated novel *The English Patient* is a lost traveler, a badly wounded man who remembers that he speaks many languages but cannot recall his name or nationality. He views the world through his battered copy of *The Histories* by Herodotus, whom the English patient sees as "one of those spare men of the desert who travel from oasis to oasis, trading legends as if it is the exchange of seeds."[5]

One common denominator in this rich variety, Whitfield says, is what travelers and readers of travelogues both seek—"what stretches our imagination and awes our mind."[6] This is what we're after—a source of awe, a surprising way of seeing, or a question not yet posed about the wild variety of being human. An "exchange of seeds." Good travel writing goes beyond reportage to excavation of meaning.

Forms of travel writing encompass personal essay, journalism, memoir, and hybrids of varied forms. "Stories Matter," an essay by Jacqui Banaszynski, is a good example of a hybrid. Banaszynski begins with "I want you to travel with me to a famine camp in Sudan." Her second-person address draws us into her experience until page 2, where she moves to first person to give the summarizing backstory: "I went to Africa in 1985 to report on the Ethiopian famine for the *St. Paul Pioneer Press*."[7] Then she shifts again a few paragraphs later to reflect on what stories mean and why we hunger for them. She quotes writer Tim O'Brien as well as coworkers in journalism that she queried about the meaning of stories. "Stories Matter" is only two and a half pages but it defies easy categorization, encompassing analytic essay, personal essay, travelogue, and journalism.

Any of the nonfiction forms in this chapter might fall under the rubric of literary travelogue if the journey offers insight to the writer, which is then conveyed to readers.

Memoir

In *Memoir: A History*, Ben Yagoda gives a historical overview of the terms "autobiography" and "memoir" and the movement toward contemporary understanding of these forms. Autobiography was and remains a full life story written by the author. "Memoirs" (plural), once synonymous with autobiography, have now given way to "memoir" (singular)—a window onto part of a life.[8] This partial story might focus on recovery from illness or a decade of political organizing or time spent in a particular place. In Peter Hessler's case, for example, his two years teaching English in China as a Peace Corps volunteer were the foundation for the widely praised *River Town: Two Years on the Yangtze*.

The Peace Corps memoir, in fact, has come into its own as a nonfiction subgenre. Some of the best works include those by Hessler, Susan Lowerre, George Packer, Sarah Erdman, and Paul Theroux. Every year many more Peace Corps memoirs are self-published. The Peace Corps Worldwide website (www.peacecorpsworldwide .org), run by the writer and former Peace Corps staffer John Coyne, promotes the writing of returned volunteers in all genres and includes book awards for nonfiction, fiction, and poetry. Coyne aims to keep alive one of the principle Peace Corps goals: for volunteers to bring home what they learned abroad "to share with all who have a desire for international understanding."[9]

Prior to the final decades of the twentieth century, many memoirs were written by celebrities and "great" historical actors. Most were men, though the novelist Edith Wharton pioneered the travel memoir—a good example of which is *Fighting France: From Dunkerque to Belfort* (1915) about her travels as a Red Cross worker on the western front in France during World War I. Wharton borrowed field glasses to witness a battle unfold in the Forest of Argonne. She wrote: "The rush of French infantry up the slopes, the feathery drift of French gun-smoke lower down, and, high up, on the wooded crest along the sky, the red lightnings and white puffs of the German artillery. Rap, rap, rap, went the answering guns, as the troops swept up and disappeared into the fire-tongued wood; and we stood there dumbfounded at the accident of having stumbled on this visible episode of the great subterranean struggle."[10] Until that moment, few women were doing that kind of writing from the frontlines.

The second wave of feminism, the civil rights movement, and eventually, the struggle for LGBT rights sent writers to their desks and computers to record their experience of these radical social shifts. Many of these memoirs celebrated unacknowledged lives, moving the genre away from the rarified world of the famous. In *Writing the Memoir: From Truth to Art,* Judith Barrington recounts how she found inspiration in feminism and the struggle for gay rights. "I was able to witness how the social movements we created, movements whose members have previously been marginalized or invisible in literature, brought about radical changes in both our determination to tell our stories and in our access to publishing."[11] The memoir explosion continues. Ben Yagoda records a 400 percent increase in memoirs published in the United States between 2004 and 2008.[12] The form and its practitioners keep shifting, with new authors emerging every year.

From another perspective, memoirs of lesser-known or disenfranchised individuals date back to early Christian stories and slave narratives. Toni Morrison prompts important questions about how to read the stories of slaves. What could slaves really tell of their lives? What would nineteenth-century readers be willing to believe? "Over and over," Morrison relates, "the writers pull the narrative up short with a phrase such as, 'But let us drop a veil over these proceedings too terrible to relate.' In shaping the experience to make it palatable to those who were in a position to alleviate it, they were silent about many things, and they 'forgot' many other things."[13] Fiction, argues Morrison, liberates the writer to lift that veil and offer more depth and accuracy about slavery's brutality.

The "memory" in memoir creates challenges. A blog or e-mail or short magazine piece written while traveling keeps you close to the facts. But details grow fuzzy if you're writing months or years later—the best argument for keeping careful journals. But even with documentation, questions come up. You noted that your friend Lydia attended that event with you, along with that man . . . who was he? The temptation to invent has ruined more than one memorist. *Three Cups of Tea: One Man's Mission to Promote Peace One School at a Time*, Greg Mortenson's wildly successful story of establishing schools in Afghanistan, won him instant fame. But less than five years after its 2007 publication, an investigative report by Jon Krakauer found enormous discrepancies and some downright fabrications. Additionally, Mortenson was accused of mismanaging funds donated to his nonprofit, seriously undermining his credibility. Krakauer's e-book, *Three Cups of Deceit: How Greg Mortenson, Humanitarian Hero, Lost His Way*, dug deeper into the accusations.

Troubling questions about memoir's reliability also appeared after the 2003 publication of James Frey's *A Million Little Pieces*, the ostensibly true story of his recovery from alcohol and drug abuse. Having failed to publish the book as a novel, he repackaged it as memoir. But many of the book's events proved fictional, triggering a literary scandal that included Frey's public dressing down by Oprah. What does all of this confusion do to reader's understanding of genre?

These controversies highlight a critical reminder: nonfiction rests on an implicit pact between author and reader. The reader's faith assumes the writer's commitment to fact-checking, vital to representing cultures unfamiliar to readers. Equally essential is fidelity to the emotional truth of memory. (See chapter 5 for a discussion of re-creating dialogue and related issues.)

The structures of memoirs vary tremendously. One classic approach is a narrative arc, which also shapes many of the stories in literary fiction, television shows, drama, and film. Across the arc, a story builds and creates tension, then reaches a climax followed by falling action and resolution. A traveler's narrative arc might look like this: an opening marked by the initial confusion of life abroad, followed by a crisis (loss of possessions or confidence, illness, or any of travel's "travails"), winding down to the traveler's discovery of (latent resilience, lost love, or some previously hidden meaning). In travel literature, the arc invites the reader on a geographic, intellectual, spiritual, or emotional journey toward that final aha moment. An arc provides a well-thumbed map.

Writing Exercise Two

Go back to a moment of confusion that you recorded. It might be the inability to grasp some experience (chapters 2 and 7), humiliation learning a language (chapter 3) or getting physically lost (chapter 6). Create an arc starting with that freewrite, then find the moment of change or transformation. Freewrite on that moment. If that big revelation never happened, write about how you imagine it would have unfolded. Begin with "If only I'd known . . ." or "If only I'd understood . . ." Add a third freewrite, starting with "Looking back now . . ."

Essay

In chapter 1, we introduced the essay by its French root— "essayer"—to try. The essayist reaches for some universal aspect of human experience yet the voice is intimate and often self-deprecating, insisting "I'm not an expert but . . ." The form is so varied that we could fill a volume with exercises; many such books exist. The continuum stretches from the formal essay of ideas to the personal essay that blurs into memoir. Mary Paumier Jones once compared the movement of essays to the meandering of rivers: "A particular essay's shape may be more akin to one of the other basic natural forms—a sphere or hexagon, a spiral, say, or helix, or branch—but on the whole, I think, what essays do best is meander."[14] Your essay may move along the classic narrative arc that many memoirs follow or hew to one of the meandering forms Jones suggests.

In *The Art of the Personal Essay*, Philip Lopate, a master practitioner, traces the history and cross-cultural occurrence of essays. He includes early Chinese and Japanese writers as well as European and North American examples. Some preceded and others followed Michel de Montaigne, the sixteenth-century writer acknowledged as the originator of the form as we know it. Montaigne followed his own mind, circling wide-ranging topics, telling stories along the way. Lopate's table of contents lists essay by theme as well as form, including diary or journal entry, list, letter (epistolary essay), mosaic (segmented or lyric essay), and portrait and double portrait, among others. Lopate incorporates memoir into his list, revealing its close kinship to personal essay.

Another useful guide to the genre's rich variety is *The Best American Essays*, an annual anthology edited by Robert Atwan and a different guest editor each year. A similar anthology is now published in Australia. Below, we examine a few of the essay's formal possibilities.

The Formal Essay. The mention of "formal" essay may suggest that five-paragraph model you hated in high school. But you can push the boundaries of old standards. You might start with a thesis, follow with an exploration of three or four connected ideas, then draw a conclusion. Nothing forbids you from telling stories. Montaigne would applaud. Many formal essays build on a central idea: the importance of environmental conservation, why indigenous languages matter, the meaning of silence for Quakers. Many are written in the third person, which doesn't mean the writer must sacrifice a personal voice. Lewis Lapham, the former editor of *Harper's Magazine*, once wrote: "On first opening a book I listen for the sound of the human voice. By this device I am absolved from reading much of what is published in a given year." Lapham liberated himself from work written in "institutional codes (academic, literary, political, bureaucratic, technical), in which they send messages already deteriorating into the half-life of yesterday's news."[15] Making an argument or exploring an issue still demands a human voice.

Formal essays can highlight contrasting or multiple points of view or illuminate cross-cultural differences. You can include quotes, research, and other materials that support or challenge diverse perspectives.

✔

Writing Exercise Three

Choose a topic you've written about in your journal, say, pollution in Chinese cities or political parties in England or gay rights in Indonesia. Begin with a statement of the issue or problem. In the course of the essay, include the following points: a related story of something that happened while you were abroad; quotes from people on both sides; and at least two questions about the issue.

This I Believe. Some essayists explore a subject using the first person, creating a bridge between personal and formal essays. A good example comes from NPR's *This I Believe* radio series. These short essays range from intimate to formal. A majority begin with "this I believe," though some open with a story and weave in an argument or set of ideas.

Here are two examples. "The Holy Life of the Intellect" by Canadian poet George Bowering opens: "I believe that the human intellect is the closest thing we have to the divine. It is the way we can join one another in spirit. Sometimes when you are listening to a great jazz musician performing a long solo, you are experiencing his mind, moment by moment, as it shifts and decides, as it adds and reminds."[16] Bowering muses about jazz, blending in quotes from Shelley and Saint Paul's Letter to the Corinthians. In contrast, "Opening the Door of Mercy" by Karin Round begins: "One afternoon a couple of summers ago, just as the sky was darkening, a woman I didn't know stood sagging on our threshold, holding the screen door open. I saw the silhouette of her head through the

window."[17] Round doesn't arrive at her belief statement until near
the end.

Writing Exercise Four

Begin with a "this I believe" statement. This may or may not be your
opening. Write a one-page essay, including at least one story and one
statement of belief. Then flip the order. If you opened with a story and
moved toward a declaration of belief, start with the statement and ease
into the story. As you revise, you may move away from the formula and
develop your unique way of expressing belief.

The Mosaic. Let's return to a mosaic or segmented essay as we
discussed in chapter 3. This subgenre is sometimes called "lyric"
essay because it combines poetry and prose. Images, metaphors,
and other poetic devices dominate, with narrative in the backseat,
if present. Ideas are suggested rather than explained, linked or
"braided" rather than expounded. The terms "collage" or "mosaic"
also apply because self-contained elements are juxtaposed without
formal transitions between them. Often, divisions between segments are marked with asterisks or roman numerals, subtitles, or
even phrases from poetry or music. Rebecca McClanahan's essay
"The Riddle Song" organizes around the lines of the well-known
folk song that begins "I gave my love a cherry that had no stone."
Mosaics allow the writer to move around in time and space, but
layout is critical. Writer and teacher Robert Root underscores the
importance of white spaces. "The segmented essay," he argues, "is
like an oratorio or a concerto. The spaces are like the intervals of
silence between the separate elements."[18]

Consider the mosaic essay "Grammar Lessons: The Subjunctive Mood," by Michelle Morano. She constructs her essay around
numbered rules for the use of the subjunctive in Spanish. Her

second-person voice speaks directly to the reader: "Think of it this way: learning to use the subjunctive mood is like learning to drive a stick shift."[19] The "you" refers to Morano herself in memory but also to us, the readers. Here is her rule number 6 for the subjunctive: "6. To Express Good Wishes *Que tengas muy buen viaje,* Lola will say, kissing each of your cheeks before leaving you off at the bus station. *May you have a good trip.* A hope, a wish, a prayer of sorts, even without the *ojalá.* The bus ride from Oviedo to Madrid is nearly six hours, so you have a lot of time for imagining."[20]

Through each numbered grammar point, Morano juxtaposes her experiences in Spain with memories of the suicidal boyfriend she left behind in the United States. Her elegant structure mixes humor with grief and keeps us on our toes trying to figure out the rules.

✔

Writing Exercise Five

Following Morano, make a list of linguistic or cultural rules. You might start with items such as: "Always use the reflexive verb for . . ." or "Never state anything directly" or "Wait for someone to offer you food." Tell a story connected to each one until you have a full draft. Reread to see if the sequence works and where the heart of the story is.

As we've noted before, when you publish a piece of writing that imitates an explicit structure such as Morano's, you need to cite that work or change the structure significantly. Imitation is useful, and yes, the highest form of flattery. But unless you remove that scaffolding or alter the piece, you're copying someone else's ideas or words without proper attribution—otherwise known as plagiarism.

A Strategy: Comparison and Contrast. At the end of chapter 7, we discussed Elizabeth Graver's essay, "Two Baths." Graver uses two travel experiences separated in time to create contrast, dividing the essay into two parts. As she moves around in time and space, we follow easily because the simplicity of this structure gives us something to hang onto. This sort of division works for any topic. But another way to create a comparison/contrast is to juxtapose elements as you go along. For example, Italian writer Natalia Ginzburg's essay "He and I" provides a double portrait that begins, "He always feels hot, I always feel cold. In the summer when it really is hot he does nothing but complain about how hot he feels. He is irritated if he sees me put a jumper on in the evening."[21] Almost every paragraph opens with a contrast, folding in more stories as the piece progresses. By the end, we feel the rich, contradictory nature of human connection.

Writing Exercise Six

Revisit your journals and chose two passages that invite comparison and contrast—perhaps a border crossing into a country and later, the crossing out. Or maybe your first taste of taro root in the Philippines opposed to your favorite meal on returning home. You might pair portraits of two people you met while traveling. Add material to expand each freewrite.

Diary Essays. More than raw material and a record of your travels, a diary, carefully revised and edited, can be a literary form. Nigerian writer Wole Soyinka's "Why Do I Fast?" provides one model, alternating musings on life and death with minute details about the tedium of prison life: "Tenth day of fast. By day a speck of dust on a sunbeam. By night a slow shuttle in the cosmos."[22] Diaries kept by a range of writers are plentiful in travel literature. James Boswell published *The Journal of a Tour to the Hebrides with Samuel Johnson, LL.D.* in 1785, whetting the public appetite for the now-famous biography that followed. Ernesto "Che" Guevara's *The Motorcycle Diaries* charts his journey through some of the poorest parts of Latin America, tracing his transformation from upper-middle-class medical student to committed revolutionary. Guevara's work exemplifies the importance of observation in keeping journals, where self-absorption always threatens. But if you've kept your lens turned outward, you'll find the potential for literary form hidden in your daily recordings.

Journalism

Traditional journalism is characterized by an objective third-person voice and the established formula of who, what, when, where, why, and how. The "lede," or first few sentences, hooks the reader and sets up the piece. The "nut graf" that follows, usually in the next paragraph, explains the topic. Newspapers and some journals still rely on this traditional format. But as we've discussed, New Journalism as well as the rise of social media and immersion journalism, have challenged established conventions. Still, you may find yourself in the midst of a social movement, a newsworthy event, or some situation that calls for a traditional reporting style.

Let's return to the *This I Believe* essays. Here's a way to continue that exercise toward a journalistic piece that you might submit to a local magazine at home, your college alumni publication, or to a news outlet.

Writing Exercise Seven

Focus on the topic you wrote about in *This I Believe*. Put aside your own beliefs and write a nut graf—a statement that clearly defines the issue. Then write an objective lede for a story, as in "The politics of same-sex marriage in Mexico City." Interview at least two people with opposing perspectives on the issue. Then read at least two news pieces and incorporate quotes and related contemporary news to shape the story with background and context.

Immersion journalism, as we've discussed, involves extended periods of time in a place and observational techniques akin to ethnography. Such work stands between the third-person reportage of traditional journalism and the self-discovery of memoir. The writer includes his or her presence and point of view. But as Ted Conover points out in *Immersion: A Writer's Guide to Going Deep,* personal revelation is secondary to the real topic. He cites Barbara Ehrenreich's *Nickel and Dimed.* The author found jobs doing minimum-wage work in the United States to expose economic inequality, but her focus stays on the waitresses and housekeepers she works with. Her book is one example of "undercover" journalism—a topic Conover explores in depth—but she writes, "This is not a story of some death-defying 'undercover' adventure. Almost anyone could do what I did—look for jobs, work those jobs, try to make ends meet. In fact, millions of Americans do it every day, and with a lot less fanfare and dithering."[23] Another example is Jan Morris's *Trieste and the Meaning of Nowhere.* A traditional journalistic work might focus on the Italian city of Trieste—a worthy objective. But an immersion piece could be, as Robin Hemley notes of Morris's book, "about the fragility of identity."[24]

CRAFT DISCUSSION: LOCAL LITERARY FORMS

Genres feel eternal and "just so." When we pick up a novel, we have expectations as readers: it will contain invented elements, be at least a certain length, and will tell a story, though perhaps not in linear fashion. Some of the great disruptions in literary history—*Ulysses,* among others—jilted reader expectations. Innovation often upsets our genre boundaries.

In chapter 1, we suggested researching the literary traditions of the place where you were headed, followed by bookstore sleuthing and interviews once you arrived. You may have discovered that genres are not eternal or universal. "Shakespeare in the Bush" is a widely anthologized article that details genre confusion and disruption. In the 1960s, anthropologist Laura Bohannan, who also wrote under the name Elenore Smith Bowen, brought a copy of *Hamlet* with her to live among the Tiv in Nigeria. Her initial attempt to explain the story prompted incredulity. Why, people asked, can't Claudius marry his brother's wife? This custom was perfectly acceptable to the Tiv. They also found the appearance of Hamlet's father's ghost perplexing because a spirit could only have been an omen sent by a witch. Some anthropologists now challenge Bohannan's story as too rigidly "us versus them," unable to account for variable responses among the Tiv. But the essay remains instructive in raising questions about how cultures read meaning. Bohannan chastises herself for assuming the universality of Shakespeare, and her humility draws us in. Readers appreciate a vulnerable, imperfect narrator.

Forms of writing in other cultures may upset accepted boundaries in U.S. literature. Consider the Mexican *crónica*, which combines fiction and nonfiction, literature and journalism. *Crónicas* appear in Mexico City newspapers and others around the country, part of a longer history in Latin American letters. Literary scholar Beth Ellen Jörgensen describes *crónicas*/chronicles as akin to news reporting in claiming to be factual. But as a hybrid genre, the *crónica* "freely borrows characteristics of the short story, the essay and the ethnographic narrative in offering a perspective that frequently runs counter to official or authorized versions of events."[25] *Crónicas* blur boundaries that U.S. writers find sacrosanct, especially the fact/fiction divide. Remember the controversies discussed above over *Three Cups of Tea* and other books.

REVISION

We've suggested numerous ways to revise in each chapter, then more extensively in chapter 9. At some point during or after your travels, you'll be ready to complete a book or essay or some other form. Deciding what "final" actually means can be challenging. Many writers feel their work is never complete; another revision might tweak a sentence that feels off or changes a comma that could shift emphasis. "Final" may be defined by an editor or a professor's deadline; sometimes we simply can't push the work further. But before you decide on "final," consider an experiment with other genres. One way to see your work anew, following Patti Smith, is to play with form as you assess what appears to be the final draft.

Experiment with Form—Try a Local Genre

Begin with a recorded experience from your journal or a freewrite to use as the basis of a new genre. Even if you don't normally write fiction, try a Mexican *crónica* by reporting on an event, then adding a fictional element. Read to listeners or send to readers and ask for responses to your blurred boundaries. Be sure to explain your experiment. A Mexican friend might shrug at adding fictional elements, while an American could object.

Whether you're a student in an overseas program or a professional journalist on assignment, you can't always predict what form your writing will take. Anne Fadiman's award-winning book *The Spirit Catches You and You Fall Down* began as a long article for the *New Yorker*. When the magazine rejected it, Fadiman was distraught at the thought of telling the Hmong family and community who'd given so much of their time that it was all for naught. "I couldn't say that one sentence. So I wrote a 300-page book instead," she said. "It was so much easier."[26]

The transformation we experience through travel and cultural immersion intensifies the need to shape experience into story. But sometimes the writer's task seems monumental. Anguished over Robert Mapplethorpe's death, Patti Smith wrote at the end of her memoir, *Just Kids*, "Why can't I write something that would wake the dead? That pursuit is what burns me most deeply."[27] Every writer struggles to create just the right form. But if we learn from Smith's passion for hard work and experimentation, Fadiman's commitment and flexibility, and the insights offered by many other writers, we'll create writing powerful enough to move our readers, if not wake the dead.

ACKNOWLEDGMENTS

We thank senior editor Mary Laur for her belief in this project and her enthusiasm, patience, and prompt attention to our questions and concerns. Acquisitions assistant Susan Zakin offered editing expertise and thoughtfully shepherded the manuscript through the production process. We are grateful to manuscript editor Yvonne Zipter for her thoughtful questions and scrupulous attention to detail. Readers Jordana Dym and Brian Whalen contributed valuable insights and suggestions for revision.

Larry Meyers, former director of Lewis and Clark College's Overseas and Off-Campus Programs, first suggested the idea for this book and consistently encouraged us. Dr. Michael Woolf of CAPA, the Global Education Network, urged us forward and shared his important writing on study abroad. Thanks to both for the opportunity to teach a writing workshop at the Forum on Education Abroad conference in San Diego, California, April 2–4, 2014.

We are deeply grateful to the many friends, colleagues, and family members who helped bring this book to fruition. For reading and responding to parts or all of the manuscript, Joanne would like to thank Andrea Carlisle, Melissa Madenski, Ben Moorad, Patricia Mulcahy, Karen Rodriguez, and Holly Sylvester. Ian McCluskey and Guha Shankar provided crucial feedback on documentary work. She owes the deepest debt to her husband Bob Hazen for his unending patience and generous response to multiple versions of the manuscript.

Joanne gratefully acknowledges the teachers and writers at the Northwest Writing Institute of Lewis and Clark College and the Bard College Institute for Writing and Thinking. Her understanding of the writing process and many of the exercises in this book grew from collaboration with colleagues in both places.

Peter thanks his partner Laura Gephart for her gracious feedback. Scott Olsen, editor of the literary journal *Ascent* and professor of English at Concordia College in Moorhead, Minnesota, provided valuable insights. Peter also thanks his writing group of fellow Washington State University colleagues for their generous help. They are Debbie Lee, Rebecca Goodrich, Bryan Fry, Julie Titone, and Larry Hufford. Roger Whitson, scholar of digital humanities and nineteenth-century literature, gave expert feedback on chapter 8, "Travel Writing and the Age of the Internet." Aaron Oforlea, also a literature professor at Washington State University, generously shared his knowledge of African American travel writing.

Finally, Joanne and Peter would like to thank the United States Fulbright Scholar Program and the Pulitzer Center on Crisis Reporting, respectively, for supporting their travel and research in Mexico and Mali.

NOTES

Introduction

1. Cynthia Ozick, "Toward a New Yiddish," in *Art and Ardor* (New York: Knopf, 1983), 154.
2. Daniel Boorstin, "From Traveler to Tourist: The Lost Art of Travel," in *The Image; or, What Happened to the American Dream* (New York: Athenaeum, 1962), 85.
3. Ibid., 87.
4. Peter Whitfield, *Travel: A Literary History* (Oxford: Bodleian Library, 2011), 283.
5. Peter Elbow, *Writing without Teachers* (New York: Oxford University Press, 1973), 3.
6. Whitfield, *Travel*, 38.
7. Michael Woolf, "The Drama of Alteration: Writing and Education Abroad," *Writing on the Edge* 24, no. 1 (Fall 2013): 80.
8. Graham Greene, *The Lawless Roads* (New York: Penguin Classics, 2005), 23.
9. Whitfield, *Travel*, 286.

Chapter 1

1. Flaubert is quoted in Guy de Maupassant, *Pierre et Jean*, trans. Julie Mead (New York: Oxford University Press, 2001), 12.

2. Gordon Lish is quoted in David Comfort, *An Insider's Guide to Publishing* (Cincinnati, OH: Writer's Digest Books, 2013), 106.

3. Francine du Plessix Gray, "The Art of Fiction No. 96," interview by Regina Weinreich, *Paris Review*, no. 103 (Summer 1987).

4. Terry Tempest Williams, "A Letter to Deb Clow," in *Red: Passion and Patience in the Desert* (New York: Vintage Books, 2002), 115.

5. Julie Checkoway, *Little Sister: Searching for the Shadow World of Chinese Women* (New York: Penguin Books, 1996), 6.

6. Raymond Williams, *Keywords: A Vocabulary of Culture and Society* (New York: Oxford University Press, 1976), 76.

7. Edward B. Tylor, *Primitive Culture: Researches into the Development of Mythology, Philosophy, Religion, Language, Art, and Custom* (New York: Cambridge University Press, 2010), 1.

8. Raymond Williams, *Resources of Hope: Culture, Democracy, Socialism* (New York: Verso, 1989), 4.

9. Clifford Geertz, *The Interpretation of Cultures* (New York: Basic Books, 1973), 49, 5.

10. Alison Buckholtz, "To Hold, Not to Have," *New York Times*, May 19, 2002, http://www.nytimes.com/2002/05/19/travel/to-hold-not-to-have.html.

11. Checkoway, *Little Sister*, 2.

12. David Duncan, *River Teeth: Stories and Writings* (New York: Doubleday, 1995), 4.

13. Pico Iyer, "Before the Fall," in *The Best Spiritual Writing*, ed. Philip Zaleski (San Francisco: Harper, 2000), 182.

14. Margaret Mead, "A Way of Seeing," in *Maiden Voyages: Writings of Women Travelers*, ed. Mary Morris (New York: Vintage, 1993), 276.

15. Matthew Desmond, *Evicted: Poverty and Profit in the American City* (New York: Crown Publishers, 2016), 317–18.

16. Ibid., 2, 328.

17. Lauren Kessler, "The Search for Meaning," *Writer's Digest* 78, no. 4 (April 1998): 34.

18. Robin Hemley, *A Field Guide to Immersion Writing: Memoir, Journalism, and Travel* (Athens: University of Georgia Press, 2012), 8. See also Ted Conover, *Immersion: A Writer's Guide to Going Deep* (Chicago: University of Chicago Press, 2016).

19. Margaret Atwood, "A View from Canada," in *Ourselves among Others: Cross-Cultural Readings for Writers*, ed. Carol J. Verburg, 3rd ed. (Boston: Bedford Books of St. Martin, 1994), 33.

20. Jamaica Kincaid, *A Small Place* (New York: Farrar, Straus, and Giroux, 2000), 4.

21. Michael Woolf, "The Baggage They Carry: Study Abroad and the Construction of 'Europe' in the American Mind," *Frontiers: The Interdisciplinary*

Journal of Study Abroad 21 (Fall 2011): 289–309, quotes on 289, 306, http:// frontiersjournal.org/wp-content/uploads/2015/09/WOOLF-FrontiersXXI -TheBaggageTheyCarry.pdf.

22. Tim O'Brien, *The Things They Carried* (Boston: Houghton Mifflin Harcourt, 2009), 20.

23. Peter Whitfield, *Travel: A Literary History* (Oxford: Bodleian Library, 2011), 78.

24. Thea Pitman, *Mexican Travel Writing* (Oxford: Peter Lang, 2008), 11.

25. David Mikics, ed., *The Annotated Emerson* (Cambridge, MA: Belknap Press of Harvard University Press, 2012), 161.

26. Gail Godwin, "The Watcher at the Gate," *New York Times,* January 9, 1977.

27. Twyla Tharp, *The Creative Habit: Learn It and Use It for Life* (New York: Simon and Schuster, 2006), 6–7.

Chapter 2

1. Ernestine McHugh, *Love and Honor in the Himalayas* (Philadelphia: University of Pennsylvania Press, 2001), 3.

2. Ibid., 3–4.

3. Ibid., 4.

4. Carlos Fuentes, *Myself with Others: Selected Essays* (New York: Farrar, Straus, and Giroux, 1990), 12.

5. William Stafford, *Writing the Australian Crawl* (Ann Arbor: University of Michigan Press, 1978), 17.

6. Barbara Sjoholm, *The Palace of the Snow Queen: Winter Travels in Lapland* ([Emeryville, CA]: Shoemaker & Hoard, 2007), 3.

7. James Baldwin, "Equal in Paris," in *Collected Essays* (New York: Library of America, 1998), 103, 102.

8. James Baldwin, "Encounter on the Seine: Black Meets Brown," in *Notes of a Native Son* (New York: Beacon, 1955), 120.

9. Baldwin, "Equal in Paris," 106, 107.

10. Ibid., 116.

11. McHugh, *Love and Honor in the Himalayas,* 14.

12. Susan Orlean, "Morocco's Extraordinary Donkeys," *Smithsonian Magazine,* September 2009, http://www.smithsonianmag.com/travel/moroccos -extraordinary-donkeys-40973739/?story=fullstory&page=3.

13. Alden Jones, "Lard Is Good for You," in *The Best American Travel Writing 2000,* ed. Bill Bryson (Boston: Houghton Mifflin, 2000), 108.

14. Karen McCarthy Brown, "Papa Ogou, Do You Take This Woman?" in *Searching for Your Soul: Writers of Many Faiths Share Their Personal Stories of Spiritual Discovery,* ed. Katherine Kurs (New York: Schocken Books, 1999), 396.

15. Ibid., 399.

16. McHugh, *Love and Honor in the Himalayas*, 60.
17. Patricia Hampl, "Pilgrim," in *The Best American Spiritual Writing 2005*, ed. Philip Zaleski (Boston: Houghton Mifflin, 2005), 103.
18. Matt Hackett, "As We Become Cameras," Medium, https://medium.com/@mhkt/as-we-become-cameras-ac142f9a8bb5#.9448k117q.
19. Sonja Dahl, "Nongkrong and Collectivity in Yogyakarta's Contemporary Arts: In Support of Non-Productive Time," paper presented at the 1st PARSE Biennial Research Conference on Time, University of Gothenburg, Sweden, November 6, 2015, 1–2.
20. Terence O'Donnell, *Garden of the Brave in War: Recollections of Iran* (Washington, DC: Mage Publishers, 2013), 88.
21. Ibid., 91.
22. Francine Prose, *Reading Like a Writer* (New York: HarperCollins, 2006), 198.
23. Leslie Jamison, "Why Do We Hate Cliché?" *New York Times*, January 6, 2015, 50–51.
24. McHugh, *Love and Honor in the Himalayas*, 169.

Chapter 3

1. Ian Frazier, *Travels in Siberia* (New York: Farrar, Straus and Giroux, 2010), 153.
2. Ibid., 143.
3. Frank Bures, "How Do You Say," *Smart Set*, November 12, 2010, http://thesmartset.com/article11121001/.
4. Ibid.
5. Paul Theroux, *Sir Vidia's Shadow* (New York: Houghton Mifflin, 1998), 25.
6. Penny Nelson, "Paul Theroux: 'The Last Train to Zona Verde,'" *Forum*, KQED Radio, San Francisco: May 17, 2013, https://ww2.kqed.org/forum/2013/05/17/paul-theroux-the-last-train-to-zona-verde/.
7. Charles Darwin, *Voyage of the HMS Beagle Round the World*, 1:264–65, quoted in Peter Whitfield, *Travel: A Literary History* (Oxford: Bodleian Library, 2011), 194.
8. Deborah Tannen, *You Just Don't Understand: Women and Men in Conversation* (New York: William Morrow), 2007.
9. Janet Holmes and Miriam Myerhoff, eds., *The Handbook of Language and Gender* (Oxford: Blackwell Publishing, 2003).
10. Deborah Fallows, *Dreaming in Chinese: Mandarin Lessons in Life, Love, and Language* (New York: Walker and Co., 2010), 44.
11. Ibid., 15.
12. Peter Chilson, *Riding the Demon: On the Road in West Africa* (Athens, Georgia: University of Georgia Press). Part of this quote appears in Peter's personal research notes and part in *Riding the Demon*, 47.
13. Frazier, *Travels in Siberia*, 105.

14. Whitfield, *Travel: A Literary History*, 198.
15. Ibid.
16. Keith Basso, *Portraits of "the Whiteman": Linguistic Play and Cultural Symbols among the Western Apache* (New York: Press Syndicate of the University of Cambridge, 1979), 46–47.
17. Basso, *Portraits of "the Whiteman,"* 48.
18. Lee Gutkind, *Keep It Real: Everything You Need to Know about Researching and Writing Creative Nonfiction* (New York: W. W. Norton, 2008), 125.
19. Paul Theroux, "Novelist and Essayist Paul Theroux on Note Taking," *Wall Street Journal*, May 3, 2013, http://www.wsj.com/articles/SB10001424127887 323528404578452834101653910.
20. F. Scott Fitzgerald, *The Great Gatsby*, in *The Cambridge Edition of the Works of F. Scott Fitzgerald* (Cambridge: Cambridge University Press), 67.
21. Joan Didion, "Some Dreamers of the Golden Dream," in *Slouching toward Bethlehem* (1961; repr., New York: Farrar, Straus, and Giroux, 1990), 3.
22. Nicholas Delbanco, *The Sincerest Form* (New York: McGraw Hill, 2003), xxi.
23. Frazier, *Travels in Siberia*, 357.
24. Ibid.
25. Johann Wolfgang Von Goethe, *Maxims and Reflections of Goethe*, trans. Bailey Saunders (New York: Macmillan, 1906), 414.
26. Toni Morrison, "Nobel Lecture," November 7, 1993, http://www.nobelprize .org/nobel_prizes/literature/laureates/1993/morrison-lecture.html.

Chapter 4

1. James Agee and Walker Evans, *Let Us Now Praise Famous Men* (Boston: Houghton Mifflin, 1980), 13.
2. Ibid., 11.
3. Robert Coles, *Doing Documentary Work* (New York: Oxford University Press, 1997), 145.
4. Duncan Murrell, "Why Documentary Writing? A Modest Proposal, with Reference to REM, Trains, Bells, and Treehouses," *Document*, the Center for Documentary Studies, June 13, 2012, 4.
5. See Gretchen Garner, *Disappearing Witness: Change in Twentieth-Century American Photography* (Baltimore: Johns Hopkins University Press, 2003), xvi.
6. Linda Gordon, *Dorothea Lange: A Life beyond Limits* (New York: W. W. Norton, 2009), 406.
7. "NPPA Code of Ethics," October 4, 2012, https://nppa.org/code_of_ethics.
8. John McPhee, "Elicitation," *New Yorker*, April 7, 2014, 50.
9. Robert S. Boynton, "Jon Krakauer," in *The New New Journalism* (New York: Vintage Books, 2005), 173.

10. McPhee, "Elicitation," 50.

11. Alessandro Portelli, "What Makes Oral History Different?" in *The Death of Luigi Trastulli, and Other Stories: Form and Meaning in Oral History* (Albany: State University of New York Press, 1991), 50.

12. Scott Pennington and Dean Rehberger, "Quick Tips for Better Interview Video," in *Oral History in the Digital Age*, ed. Doug Boyd, Steve Cohen, Brad Rakerd, and Dean Rehberger (Washington, DC: Institute of Museum and Library Services, 2012), http://ohda.matrix.msu.edu/2012/08/quick-tips-for -better-interview-video/.

13. See Dell H. Hymes, *"In vain I tried to tell you": Essays in Native American Ethnopoetics* (Philadelphia: University of Pennsylvania Press, 1981); poet and translator Jerome Rothenberg, *Technicians of the Sacred* (New York: Anchor/ Doubleday, 1969); and Dennis Tedlock, *The Spoken Word and the Work of Interpretation* (Philadelphia: University of Pennsylvania Press, 1983). Rothenberg and Tedlock also edited the ethnopoetics journal *Alcheringa* through Boston University from 1970 to 1980 (http://jacket2.org/reissues/alcheringa).

14. Shirley Miller Sherrod, interview by Joseph Mosnier, September 15, 2011, Civil Rights History Project Interview completed by the Southern Oral History Program under contract to the Smithsonian Institution's National Museum of African American History & Culture and the Library of Congress, http://1.usa.gov/1WvofCg.

15. Doug Boyd, Danielle Gabbard, Sara Price, and Alana Boltz, "Indexing Interviews in OHMS: An Overview," in *Oral History in the Digital Age*, ed. Doug Boyd, Steve Cohen, Brad Rakerd, and Dean Rehberger (Washington, DC: Institute of Museum and Library Services, 2014), http://ohda.matrix.msu .edu/2014/11/indexing-interviews-in-ohms/.

16. Mark O. Badger, Richard K. Nelson, and John Luther Adams, *Make Prayers to the Raven* (Fairbanks, AK: KUAC, 2007), 2 DVDs. A guide summarizing the videos can be found at http://www.iupui.edu/~mstd/e320/raven.html.

17. Alex Marshall, "London, as You've Never Heard It Before," *New York Times*, August 5, 2016, http://www.nytimes.com/2016/08/06/arts/music/london-as -youve-never-heard-it-before.html?emc=edit_th_20160806&nl=todays headlines&nlid=61412542.

18. Audrey Amidon, "Film Preservation 101: What's the Difference between a Film and a Video?" *Unwritten Record* (blog), National Archives, June 25, 2013, https://unwritten-record.blogs.archives.gov/2013/06/25/film-preservation -101-whats-the-difference-between-a-film-and-a-video/.

19. Bill Nichols, *Introduction to Documentary*, 2nd ed. (Bloomington: Indiana University Press, 2010), 13.

20. "Best Videos by Peace Corps Volunteers around the World," Intentional Travelers, http://intentionaltravelers.com/videos-peace-corps-around -world/; Share Your Experience: Tips, Tools, and Resources to Share Your Experience," Peace Corps, http://www.peacecorps.gov/resources/returned /thirdgoal/tellyourstory/; and "Peace Corps Video Production Guide," Peace Corps, June 2016, http://files.peacecorps.gov/resources/returned/rpcv _video_production_guide.pdf.

21. Nancy Kalow, *Visual Storytelling: The Digital Video Documentary* (Durham, NC: Center for Documentary Studies at Duke University, 2011), http:// www.visualstorytellingonline.org/.

22. Center for Documentary Studies at Duke University, http:// documentarystudies.duke.edu/; Salt Institute for Documentary Studies, http://www.salt.edu/multimedia/faqs-salt-meca-partnership/; and "Documentary Media Studies (Graduate Certificate)," New School: Public Engagement, http://www.newschool.edu/public-engagement/documentary -media-graduate-certificate/.

23. For more on the Maasai documentary project, see Guha Shankar, "From Subject to Producer: Reframing the Indigenous Heritage through Cultural Documentation Training," *International Journal of Intangible Heritage* 5 (2010): 14–24, https://www.loc.gov/folklife/edresources/edcenter_files/IJIH _Article_small.pdf.

24. Coles, *Doing Documentary Work*, 251–52.

Chapter 5

1. Mark Doty, "Return to Sender," *Writer's Chronicle* 38, no. 2 (October–November 2005): 17.

2. Peter Hessler, "Tales of the Trash," *New Yorker*, October 13, 2014, 90.

3. Natalie Kusz, "Inscribed on the Body," *Harper's Magazine*, July 1995, 79.

4. Clifford Geertz, *The Interpretation of Culture* (New York: Basic Books, 1973), 375.

5. Howard A. Norman, *The Wishing Bone Cycle: Narrative Poems of the Swampy Cree Indians* (Santa Barbara, CA: Ross-Erikson Publishing, 1982), 57, 45.

6. David Long, "Stuff," *Poets and Writers Magazine*, September/October 2002, 23.

7. Helen Thayer, *Walking the Gobi* (Seattle, WA: Mountaineers Books, 2007), 250.

8. Hessler, "Tales of the Trash," 93.

9. Cited in Robert Atwan, "Prologue: How Nonfiction Finally Achieved Literary Status," in *I'll Tell You Mine: Thirty Years of Essays from the Iowa Nonfiction Program*, ed. Hope Edelman and Robin Hemley (Chicago: University of Chicago Press, 2015), xxii.

10. Hessler, "Tales of the Trash," 94.

11. Ibid., 99.

12. Kathleen Tyau, "How to Cook Rice," in *A Little Too Much Is Enough* (New York: W. W. Norton, 1996), 24.

13. Barbara Myerhoff, *Number Our Days* (New York: Simon and Schuster, 1978), 42.

14. Walt Harrington, "Toward an Ethical Code for Narrative Journalists," in *Telling True Stories: A Nonfiction Writers' Guide*, ed. Mark Kramer and Wendy Call (New York: Penguin, 2007), 170–72.

15. Studs Terkel, *Coming of Age: The Story of Our Century by Those Who've Lived It* (New York: New Press, 1995), 145.

16. Svetlana Alexievich, "Voices from Chernobyl," *Paris Review*, no. 172 (Winter 2004), http://www.theparisreview.org/letters-essays/5447/voices-from-chernobyl-svetlana-alexievich.

17. David Remnick, ed., *Life Stories: Profiles from the New Yorker* (New York: Modern Library, 2001), ix.

18. Chris Mohney, "The Art of the Profile with David Remnick of 'The New Yorker,'" July 23, 2012, http://storyboard.tumblr.com/post/27833267196/the-art-of-the-profile-with-david-remnick-of-the.

19. Calvin Tomkins, "The Man Who Walks on Air," in *Life Stories*, ed. Remnick, 196.

20. Philip Garrison, *Because I Don't Have Wings: Stories of Mexican Immigrant Life* (Tucson: University of Arizona Press, 2006), 97.

21. Hessler, "Tales of the Trash," 98.

22. Alec Wilkinson, *Moonshine: A Life in Pursuit of White Liquor* (St. Paul, MN: Ruminator Press, 1998), 64.

23. Alexievich, "Voices from Chernobyl."

24. Haruki Murakami, "The Art of Fiction No. 182," interview by John Wray, *Paris Review*, no. 170 (Summer 2004), http://www.theparisreview.org/interviews/2/the-art-of-fiction-no-182-haruki-murakami.

25. Hessler, "Tales of the Trash," 99.

Chapter 6

1. Bob Shacochis, in conversation with Peter Chilson, at the Port Townsend Writer's Conference, Port Townsend, WA, July 23, 2011.

2. Kirin Narayan, *Alive in the Writing* (Chicago: University of Chicago Press, 2012), 26.

3. Cynthia Ozick, "Toward a New Yiddish," in *Art and Ardor* (New York: Knopf, 1983), 154.

4. Peter Whitfield, *Travel: A Literary History* (Oxford: Bodleian Library, 2011), 243.

5. Ibid.

6. Luis Urrea, *The Devil's Highway* (New York: Little Brown, 2004), 6.

7. Graham Greene, *The Lawless Roads* (New York: Penguin Classics, 2005), 23.
8. Ibid.
9. John Noble Wilford, *The Mapmakers*, 2nd ed. (New York, Vintage Books, 2000), 3—5.
10. Wendy Call, *No Word for Welcome: The Mexican Village Faces the Global Economy* (Lincoln: University of Nebraska Press, 2011), xxi—xxii.
11. Thomas J. Bassett, "'From the Best Authorities': The Mountains of Kong in the Cartography of West Africa," *Journal of African History* 32, no. 3 (November 1991): 368.
12. Mark Monmonier, *How to Lie with Maps* (Chicago: University of Chicago Press, 1996), 1.
13. George Packer. *The Village of Waiting* (New York: Vintage Departures, 1988), 3.
14. Barry Lopez and Debra Gwartney, eds., *Homeground: Language for an American Landscape* (San Antonio, TX: Trinity University Press, 1006), 286.
15. Leslie Jamison, *The Empathy Exams* (Minneapolis, MN: Graywolf Press, 2014), 79.
16. David Sedaris, "Dentists without Borders," *New Yorker*, April 2, 2012.
17. Eddy L. Harris: *South of Haunted Dreams: A Ride Through Slavery's Old Back Yard* (New York: Simon and Schuster, 1993), 13.
18. Anton Chekhov, *How to Write Like Chekhov: Advice and Inspiration, Straight from His Own Letters and Work*, ed. Piero Brunello and Lena Lencek (Boston: Da Capo Press, 2008), 30.
19. "Southern Exposure," interview with Sara Wheeler, in *A Sense of Place: Travel Writers and Their Craft*, ed. Michael Shapiro (Palo Alto, CA: Travelers' Tales, 2004), 284.
20. Craig Childs, *House of Rain: Tracking a Vanished Civilization across the American Southwest* (New York: Back Bay Books, 2008), 48.
21. Andrew X. Pham, *Catfish and Mandala: A Two-Wheeled Voyage through Landscape and Memory of Vietnam* (New York: Farrar, Straus and Giroux, 1999), 302.
22. Robert Kaplan, *Balkan Ghosts: A Journey through History* (New York: Vintage Books, 1994), 35.
23. D. J. Lee, "The Edge Is What We Have," *Tinge Magazine*, no. 4 (Fall 2012), http://www.tingemagazine.org/the-edge-is-what-we-have/.
24. Urrea, *Devil's Highway*, 3—4.
25. Nancy Scheper-Hughes, *Death without Weeping: The Violence of Everyday Life in Brazil* (Berkeley: University of California Press, 1992), xii.

Chapter 7

1. George Saunders, "The Incredible Buddha Boy," in *The Best American Travel Writing 2007*, ed. Susan Orlean (Boston: Houghton Mifflin, 2007), 225.

2. Ibid., 229.

3. For a discussion of Lewis Henry Morgan, see Whitfield, *Travel: A Literary History* (Oxford: Bodleian Library, 2011), 203.

4. Saunders, "The Incredible Buddha Boy," 224.

5. Faith Adiele, *Meeting Faith: The Forest Journals of a Black Buddhist Nun* (New York: Norton, 2004), 26.

6. Ibid., 28.

7. Anne Fadiman, *The Spirit Catches You and You Fall Down* (New York: Farrar, Straus, and Giroux, 1997), viii.

8. Elias Canetti, *The Voices of Marrakesh: A Record of a Visit*, trans. J. A. Underwood (New York: Marion Boyars, 2001), 23–26.

9. Saunders, "The Incredible Buddha Boy," 229.

10. Leslie Jamison, *The Empathy Exams* (Minneapolis, MN: Graywolf Press, 2014), 154–55.

11. Angela Bourke, "More in Anger Than in Sorrow: Irish Women's Lament Poetry," in *Feminist Messages: Coding in Women's Folk Culture*, ed. Joan Newlon Radner (Urbana: University of Illinois Press, 1993), 160–82.

12. Michael T. Luongo, *Gay Travels in the Muslim World* (Binghamton, NY: Haworth Press, 2007), 11.

13. Elinor Langer, *Josephine Herbst* (Boston: Little, Brown, 1983), 166.

14. Dean MacCannell, *The Tourist: A New Theory of the Leisure Class* (Berkeley: University of California Press, 2013), 3.

15. W. Richard West Jr., quoted in Multicultural Student Affairs, "What Is Powwow?" North Carolina State University, https://oied.ncsu.edu/MSA/native-american-student-affairs/powwow/.

16. Saunders, "The Incredible Buddha Boy," 222.

17. Ibid., 224.

18. Osman Balkan, quoted in "A Home after Death," *Omnia: All Things Penn Arts and Sciences*, November 21, 2016, https://omnia.sas.upenn.edu/story/home-after-death-0.

19. David Berreby, "The Unabsolute Truths of Clifford Geertz," *New York Times Magazine*, April 9, 1995, 47.

20. Nancy Scheper-Hughes, "Death without Weeping: Has Poverty Ravaged Mother Love in the Shantytowns of Brazil?" *Natural History* 10 (October 1989): 8.

21. Stephen Kinzer, *Crescent and Star: Turkey between Two Worlds* (New York: Farrar, Straus, and Giroux, 2001), 115.

22. Ibid., 116.

23. Elizabeth Graver, "Two Baths," in *The Best American Essays 1998*, ed. Cynthia Ozick (Boston: Houghton Mifflin, 1998), 146, 152.

24. Moshin Hamid, "Bookends: What Are the Draws and Drawbacks of Success for Writers?" *New York Times Book Review*, May 13, 2014, https://www.nytimes .com/2014/05/18/books/review/what-are-the-draws-and-drawbacks-of -success-for-writers.html?_r=0.

25. Saunders, "The Incredible Buddha Boy," 245.

Chapter 8

1. Pietro Rea, "Relying on Twitter during Hurricane Sandy," *Huffington Post*, November 3, 2012, http://www.huffingtonpost.com/pietro-rea/twitter -hurricane-sandy_b_2059980.html.

2. Robert Kaplan, "Being There," *Atlantic Monthly*, November 2012, http:// www.theatlantic.com/magazine/archive/2012/11/being-there/309108/.

3. Alec Ash, "Paul Theroux on Traveling," *Salon*, June 25, 2012 http://www .salon.com/2012/06/25/paul_theroux_on_travelling_salpart/.

4. Doreen Carvajal, "In Tourist Destinations, a Picture of Excess," *New York Times*, July 11, 2015 http://www.nytimes.com/2015/07/12/world/europe /selfie-vacation-damage-majorca-paris-ibiza-rome.html.

5. @tejucole, https://twitter.com/tejucole/timelines/462974573135536128.

6. Mark Pearson, *Blogging or Tweeting without Getting Sued: A Global Guide to the Law for Anyone Writing Online* (Crows Nest, Australia: Allen and Unwin, 2012), xi.

7. Shea Bennett, "How to Write the Perfect Tweet," *SocialTimes* (blog), Ad-Week Network, July 3, 2012, http://www.adweek.com/socialtimes/the -perfect-tweet/447086?red=at.

8. "'While I was sleeping, a rat bit my face.' Migrant children detained in squalid conditions in #Thailand new @hrw rpt" (Phil Robertson [Reaproy], Twitter post, September 1, 2014, 8:55 p.m., https://twitter.com/reaproy/ status/506651594985713666.

9. Voltaire, *Philosophical Dictionary* (New York: Penguin Classics, 1984).

10. Salman Rushdie (SalmanRushdie), Twitter post, December 8, 2013, 1:53 A.M., https://twitter.com/SalmanRushdie/status/409621766370516992, in-cluding the many Tweets in reply.

11. Frances Romero, "Top Ten Twitter Controversies," *Time*, June 06, 2011, http://content.time.com/time/specials/packages/article/0,28804,2075071 _2075082_2075118,00.html.

12. Steven Kurutz, "Real Adventurers Read Maps: Using Maps vs. GPS," *New York Times*, July 14, 2014, http://www.nytimes.com/2014/07/20/opinion/ sunday/using-maps-vs-gps.html.

13. Riback, quoted in ibid.

14. Gilad Lotan, "Israel, Gaza, War and Data: Social Networks and the Art of Personalizing Propaganda," *Medium*, August 4, 2014, https://medium

.com/i-data/israel-gaza-war-data-a54969aeb23e?curator=MediaREDEF#
.pqu3rou76.

15. John Maloof, "Vivian Maier: History," http://www.vivianmaier.com/
about-vivian-maier/history/.

16. Don MacLeod. *How to Find Out Anything: From Extreme Google Searches to
Scouring Government Documents, a Guide to Uncovering Anything about Everyone
and Everything* (New York: Prentice Hall, 2012), 96.

17. Tim O'Reilly, "Draft Bloggers Code of Conduct," April 8, 2007, http://
radar.oreilly.com/2007/04/draft-bloggers-code-of-conduct.html.

18. Diane Nadin, "Is Blogging Worth Your Time Writers Bureau, May 29, 2013,
http://www.writersbureau.com/blog/blogging-worth-time/2013/05/.

19. Luke O'Neill, "The Year We Broke the Internet," *Esquire*, December 23,
2013, http://www.esquire.com/news-politics/news/a23711/we-broke-the
-internet/.

20. Andrew Sullivan, "The Years of Writing Dangerously," *Dish*, February 6,
2015, http://dish.andrewsullivan.com/2015/02/06/the-years-of-writing
-dangerously/.

21. Pew Research Center, "Twitter a Key Source of News for Many during Hurricane Sandy," November 14, 2012, http://www.pewresearch.org/daily-number/
twitter-a-key-source-of-news-for-many-during-hurricane-sandy/.

22. T. S. Eliot, *Burnt Norton* (New York: Faber and Faber, 1943).

Chapter 9

1. Cynthia Ozick, "Toward a New Yiddish," in *Art and Ardor* (New York:
Knopf, 1983), 154.

2. Winston Churchill cited in John Craig, *Peculiar Liaisons in War, Espionage, and
Terrorism in the Twentieth Century* (New York: Algora Publishing, 2004), 94;
Christopher Hitchens, "The Last of the Scholar Warriors," *Slate*, June 13, 2011.

3. Elmore Leonard, "Elmore Leonard's Ten Rules of Writers," *Guardian*, May 25,
2010, http://www.theguardian.com/books/2010/feb/24/elmore-leonard-rules
-for-writers.

4. Susan Sontag, "20 Great Writers on the Art of Revision," *Atlantic Monthly*,
January 14, 2013.

5. Dorothy Parker, "The Art of Fiction No. 13," interview by Marion Capron,
Paris Review, no. 13 (Summer 1956).

6. David Remnick, cited in Stephen Koch, *The Modern Library Writer's Workshop: A Guide to the Craft of Fiction* (New York: Modern Library, 2003), 158.

7. Anne Fadiman, *The Spirit Catches You and You Fall Down* (New York: Farrar,
Straus, and Giroux, 1997), 328.

8. Ted Conover, *Whiteout: Lost in Aspen* (New York, Vintage, 1993), 1.

9. Lewis Hyde, *The Gift: Imagination and the Erotic Life of Property* (New York: Vintage Books, 1979), 311.

10. Musa Mayer, *Night Studio: A Memoir of Philip Guston* (New York: Penguin Books, 1988), 171–72.

11. Meredith Sue Willis, *Deep Revision: A Guide for Teachers, Students, and Other Writers* (New York: Teachers and Writers Collaborative, 1993), 63.

12. Susan Bell, *The Artful Edit* (New York: W. W. Norton, 2007), 44–45.

13. Annie Dillard, *The Writing Life* (New York: Harper Perennial, 1990), 3.

14. Donald M. Murray, "Some Notes on Revision," in *FieldWorking: Reading and Writing Research*, ed. Bonnie Stone Sunstein and Elizabeth Chiseri-Strater, 4th ed. (New York: Bedford St. Martins, 2011), 381.

15. Vivian Gornick, *The Situation and the Story* (New York: Farrar, Straus, and Giroux, 2001), 13.

16. Zoë Heller, "Can Writing Be Taught?" *New York Times Book Review*, August 19, 2014.

17. Mark Twain cited in *Mark Twain at Your Fingertips: A Book of Quotations*, ed. Caroline Thomas Harnsberger (Mineola, NY: Dover Publications, 2009), 161.

18. Steven Pinker, *The Sense of Style: The Thinking Person's Guide to Writing in the 21st Century* (New York: Penguin, 2014), 3.

19. "Beige voice" is quoted in William Cane's *Write Like the Masters: Emulating the Best of Hemingway, Faulkner, Salinger, and Others* (Cincinnati, OH: Writers' Digest Books, 2009), 182.

20. Jessica Anya Blau, "Why Francine Prose No Longer Teaches Writing Workshops," *The Nervous Breakdown*, April 16, 2011, http://www
.thenervousbreakdown.com/jablau/2011/04/why-francine-prose-no-longer
-teaches-writing-workshops/.

21. Charles Dickens, *A Tale of Two Cities* (New York: Dover Publications, Inc., 1999), 1.

22. Bell, *The Artful Edit*, 118.

23. Seth Fried, "Murder Your Darlings," *The Open Bar* (blog), *Tin House*, April 15, 2013, http://www.tinhouse.com/blog/24831/murder-your-darlings.html.

24. Quote from the film, *A River Runs through It* (Culver City, CA: Tri Star Pictures, 1992).

25. Koch, *The Modern Library Writer's Workshop*, 174–75.

26. Gustav Flaubert, *Madame Bovary*, trans. Lydia Davis (New York: Penguin, 2010).

27. "Writing Group Guidelines," Writers on the Plains, last modified September 3, 2014, http://lib.colostate.edu/writersontheplains/collaborate/writing
.html.

28. "Blog It Home," Peace Corps, https://www.peacecorps.gov/returned
-volunteers/awards/blog-it-home/.

29. Adapted from Peter Elbow and Pat Belanoff, *Sharing and Responding* (New
York: Random House, 1989).

30. Debbie Lee, Professor of English, Washington State University, unpublished
essay on William Blake.

31. Scott Anderson, *Lawrence in Arabia: War, Deceit, Imperial Folly and the Making
of the Modern Middle East* (New York: Anchor Books, 2014), 504.

Chapter 10

1. Patti Smith, *Just Kids* (New York: Harper Collins, 2010), 57.

2. Ibid., 61.

3. Bill Roorbach, *Writing Life Stories: How to Make Memories into Memoirs, Ideas
into Essays, and Life into Literature* (Cincinnati, OH: Story Press, 1998), 160.

4. Peter Whitfield, *Travel: A Literary History* (Oxford: The Bodleian Library,
2011), 32.

5. Michael Ondaatje, *The English Patient* (New York: Vintage International,
1993), 118–19.

6. Whitfield, *Travel: A Literary History*, 243.

7. Jacqui Banaszynski, "Stories Matter," in *Telling True Stories: A Nonfiction Writers' Guide from the Nieman Foundation at Harvard University* (New York: Penguin,
2007), 3–4.

8. Ben Yagoda, *Memoir: A History* (New York: Riverhead Books, 2009), 1–2.

9. John Coyne, ed., Peace Corps Worldwide, http://peacecorpsworldwide.org/
about/.

10. Edith Wharton, *Fighting France: From Dunkerque to Belfort* (Toronto: McLeod
and Allen Publishers, 1915), 64.

11. Judith Barrington, *Writing the Memoir: From Truth to Art* (Portland, OR:
Eighth Mountain Press, 1997), 12.

12. Yagoda, *Memoir*, 7.

13. Toni Morrison, "The Site of Memory," in *Inventing the Truth: The Art and
Craft of Memoir*, ed. William Zinsser, 2d ed. (Boston: New York: Houghton
Mifflin, 1995), 90–91.

14. Mary Paumier Jones, "Meander," *Creative Nonfiction*, no. 50 (Fall 2013–Winter
2014), https://www.creativenonfiction.org/online-reading/meander.

15. Lewis Lapham, "On Reading," *Harper's Magazine*, May 1984, 6.

16. George Bowering, "The Holy Life of the Intellect," NPR, "This I Believe,"
August 19, 2007: http://www.npr.org/templates/story/story.php?storyId=
12821079.

17. Karin Round, "Opening the Door of Mercy," on *This I Believe*, NPR, September 10, 2010, http://thisibelieve.org/essay/14284/.

18. Robert Root, "This Is What the Spaces Say," paper presented at the Conference on College Composition and Communication Presentation, Denver, CO, March 15, 2001.

19. Michelle Morano, "Grammar Lessons: The Subjunctive Mood," in *The Best American Essays 2006*, ed. Lauren Slater, series ed. Robert Atwan (Boston: Houghton Mifflin, 2006), 107.

20. Morano, "Grammar Lessons," 115.

21. Natalia Ginzburg, "He and I," in *The Art of the Personal Essay: An Anthology from the Classical Era to the Present*, ed. Philip Lopate (New York: Anchor/ Doubleday, 1995), 423.

22. Wole Soyinka, "Why Do I Fast?" in *The Art of the Personal Essay*, ed. Lopate, 456.

23. Barbara Ehrenreich, *Nickel and Dimed: On (Not) Getting By in America* (New York: Henry Holt, 2001), 6.

24. Robin Hemley, *A Field Guide for Immersion Writing: Memoir, Journalism and Travel* (Athens: University of Georgia Press, 2012), 109.

25. Beth Ellen Jörgensen, *Documents in Crisis: Nonfiction Literatures in Twentieth-Century Mexico* (Albany, NY: SUNY Press, 2011), 141.

26. Amanda Kenyon Waite, "Author Anne Fadiman Advises First-Years on Writing, Cross-Cultural Collaboration," University Communications, September 16, 2015, University of Vermont, http://www.uvm.edu/~uvmpr/ ?Page=news&storyID=21438.

27. Smith, *Just Kids*, 279.

SELECTED BIBLIOGRAPHY

Books on Writing

Barrington, Judith. *Writing the Memoir: From Truth to Art*. Portland, OR: Eighth Mountain Press, 1997.

Boynton, Robert S. *The New New Journalism: Conversations with America's Best Nonfiction Writers on Their Craft*. New York: Vintage Books, 2005.

Burroway, Janet. *Imaginative Writing: The Elements of Craft*. New York: Longman, Inc., 2003.

Conover, Ted. *Immersion: A Writer's Guide to Going Deep*. Chicago: University of Chicago Press, 2016.

D'Agata, John, ed. *The Next American Essay*. Minneapolis: Graywolf Press, 2003.

Elbow, Peter. *Writing without Teachers*. 2nd ed. New York: Oxford University Press, 1998.

Forché, Carolyn, and Philip Gerard, eds. *Writing Creative Nonfiction*. Cincinnati, OH: Story Press, 2001.

Gutkind, Lee. *Keep It Real: Everything You Need to Know about Researching and Writing Creative Nonfiction*. New York: W. W. Norton, 2009.

Karr, Mary. *The Art of Memoir*. New York: Harper/HarperCollins, 2015.

Kidder, Tracy, and Richard Todd. *Good Prose: The Art of Nonfiction—Stories and Advice from a Lifetime of Writing and Editing*. New York: Random House, 2013.

Miller, Brenda, and Suzanne Paola. *Tell It Slant: Writing and Shaping Creative Non-fiction*. New York: McGraw-Hill, 2005.

Roorbach, Bill. *Writing Life Stories: How to Make Memories into Memoirs, Ideas into Essays, and Life into Literature*. Cincinnati, OH: Story Press, 1998.

Root, Robert. *The Nonfictionist's Guide: On Reading and Writing Creative Nonfiction*. Lanham, MD: Rowman & Littlefield Publishers, Inc., 2008.

Stafford, Kim. *The Muses among Us*. Athens: University of Georgia Press, 2003.

Zinsser, William, ed. *Inventing the Truth: The Art and Craft of Memoir*. Boston: Houghton Mifflin, 1987.

———. *On Writing Well: An Informal Guide to Writing Nonfiction*. New York: Harper & Row, 1976.

Travel Writing Collections

Bohls, Elizabeth A., and Ian Duncan, eds. *Travel Writing 1700–1830: An Anthology*. Oxford World's Classics. Oxford: Oxford University Press, 2009.

Espey, David, ed. *Writing the Journey: Essays, Stories, and Poems on Travel*. New York: Longman, 2004.

Foster, Shirley, and Sara Mills, eds. *An Anthology of Women's Travel Writing*. Manchester: Manchester University Press, 2002.

Fraser, Keath. *Bad Trips: A Sometimes Terrifying, Sometimes Hilarious Collection of Writing on the Perils of the Road*. New York: Vintage Books, 1991.

Morris, Jan. *The World: Travels, 1950–2000*. New York: Norton, 2005.

Potts, Rolf. *Vagabonding: An Uncommon Guide to the Art of Long-Term World Travel*. New York: Ballantine Books, 2002.

Spalding, Lavinia, ed. *The Best Women's Travel Writing: True Stories from Around the World*. Palo Alto, CA: Travelers' Tales, 2011–.

Theroux, Paul, ed. *The Tao of Travel: Enlightenments from Lives on the Road*. New York: Mariner Books, 2012.

Wilson, Jason, ed. *Best American Travel Writing*. Annual anthology. New York: Mariner Books, 2000–.

Books on Ethnographic Writing and Fieldwork

Clifford, James, and George Marcus, eds. *Writing Culture: The Poetics and Politics of Anthropology*. Berkeley: University of California Press, 1986.

Crane, Julia G., and Michael V. Angrosino. *Field Projects in Anthropology: A Student Handbook*. 3rd ed. Prospect Heights, IL: Waveland Press, 1992.

Emerson, Robert M., Rachel Fretz, and Linda L. Shaw. *Writing Ethnographic Fieldnotes*. Chicago: University of Chicago Press, 1995.

Geertz, Clifford. *Works and Lives: The Anthropologist as Author*. Palo Alto, CA: Stanford University Press, 1988.

Ghodsee, Kristen. *From Notes to Narrative: Writing Ethnographies That Everyone Can Read*. Chicago: University of Chicago Press, 2016.

Jackson, Bruce. *Fieldwork*. Urbana-Champaign: University of Illinois Press, 1987.

Lassiter, Luke Eric. *The Chicago Guide to Collaborative Ethnography*. Chicago: University of Chicago Press, 2005.

Narayan, Kirin. *Alive in the Writing: Crafting Ethnography in the Company of Chekhov*. Chicago: University of Chicago Press, 2012.

Sustein, Bonnie Stone, and Elizabeth Chiseri-Strater. *Fieldworking: Reading and Writing Research*. 2nd ed. New York: Bedford/St. Martin's, 2002.

Van Mannan, John. *Tales of the Field: On Writing Ethnography*. Chicago: University of Chicago Press, 1988.

INDEX

Côte d'Ivoire, 59–60, 110, 112

Coyne, John, 192

creative nonfiction, 189; essays, 195–201; journalism, 201–2; memoirs, 192–95; travel writing, 190–91. *See also* nonfiction writing

Crescent and Star (Kinzer), 49, 144

crónica, 29, 203–4

Cuba, 96–97, 135

Cultural Archive of Cañar, 86

cultural immersion, 6

cultural logic, and space, 44–45

cultural relativism, 38

culture, 18–19, 22, 38, 50; definition of, 17; and food, 39–41; and identity, 37; as kind of map, 17; and language, 54–57; and religion, 129; and technology, 150

cultures, 4–6, 35

Dahl, Sonja, 46

Darwin, Charles, 55

Davidson, Jay, 134–35

Davis, Natalie Zemon, 139

Death without Weeping (Scheper-Hughes), 143

Deep Revision (Willis), 175

Defoe, Daniel, 103

de las Casas, Bartolomé, 61

Delbanco, Nicholas, 66

"Dentists without Borders" (Sedaris), 119

Desmond, Matthew, 22–23

Devil's Highway, The (Urrea), 110–11, 125

Dickens, Charles, 181

Didion, Joan, 66

digital storytelling, 6, 84–85

Dillard, Annie, 176

Dish (blog), 164

documentaries, 82–83; documentarians, as witnesses, 86–87; documentary forms, 88–89; documentary media, 6

documentary photography, 72–75

documentary writing, 8, 15, 70–71; and storytelling, 72

Doty, Mark, 90

double consciousness, 135

DoubleTake Magazine, 75

Dreaming in Chinese (Fallows), 57

Duncan, David, 19

Eberhardt, Isabelle, 28, 134

"Edge Is What We Have, The" (Lee), 125

Egypt, 72, 96, 108, 149

Ehrenreich, Barbara, 202

Ehrlich, Gretel, 110

Elbow, Peter, 4, 18, 185, 187

Eliot, T. S., 167

Emerson, Ralph Waldo, 30

Emma Lazarus Club, 93

Engelbrecht, Beate, 83

England, 3, 19–20. *See also* Britain

English Patient, The (Ondantje), 191

"Equal in Paris" (Baldwin), 37

Erdman, Sarah, 59–60, 192

essays, 8–9, 15, 32, 49, 195; comparison and contrast essays, 199–200; diary essays, 200–201; first-person essays, 197–98; formal essays, 196–97; and journalism, 201–2; mosaic essays, 198–99

ethics, 41; environmental issues, 117–18; ethical choices, 142–43; and photography, 73–74; and portraits, 99–101

ethnography, 8–9, 22–23, 83, 100, 127

Harrington, Walt, 101
Harris, Eddy L., 119
Havana (Cuba), 96
"He and I" (Ginzburg), 200
Heller, Zoë, 179
Hemingway, Ernest, 65, 173, 183
Hemley, Robin, 23, 202
Herbst, Josephine, 135–36
Herodotus, 27, 191
Herrmann, John, 135
Hessler, Peter, 28–29, 92, 95–98, 100,
    104, 107–8, 192
Heynen, Jim, 174
historical research, and imagination,
    138–39
Histories, The (Herodotus), 191
Hitchens, Christopher, 172
Hochschild, Adam, 77
Hollywood, CA, 29
Holmes, Janet, 56
Holy Roman Empire, 122
Homeground (Lopez and Gwartney), 117
Horowitz, Tony, 123
hospitality, 41
House of Rain (Childs), 120
"How Do You Say" (Bures), 52
"How to Cook Rice" (Tyau), 99
How to Find Out Anything (MacLeod),
    158
How to Lie with Maps (Monmonier),
    115
humor, 64
Hurricane Katrina, 130
Hurricane Sandy, 148–49, 167
Hyde, Lewis, 174
Hymes, Dell, 80

Iceland, 30
identity: and culture, 37; shifting
    nature of, 39

Ignatenko, Lyudmilla, 102–3
Ignatenko, Vasily, 102
immersion, 38
Immersion (Conover), 202
immersion journalism, 6, 23, 83
"Incredible Buddha Boy, The" (Saun-
    ders), 128, 130, 132, 138, 146
India, 134, 136, 163
indigenous groups, 141
Indonesia, 46
In Morocco (Wharton), 28
"Inscribed on the Body" (Kusz), 92
Institute of Museum and Library
    Services, 79
interviews, 76, 139; index for, 79;
    and listening, 77; rules of, 78–79;
    styles of, 77; transcribing of,
    79–80
Iraq, 130, 172
Iraq war, 62–63
Ireland, 30, 134
Irving, John, 171
Islam, 140
Israel, 157
Istanbul (Turkey), 49, 146
Italy, 5
Iyer, Pico, 19–20

Jacoby, Annalee, 28
Jamison, Leslie, 48, 118, 133
Japan, 20, 139
Jesus' Son (Johnson), 48
Johnson, Denis, 48
Jones, Alden, 40–41
Jones, Mary Paumier, 195
Jones, Stephen Graham, 117
Jordan, 174
Jörgensen, Beth Ellen, 203
journalism, 49, 65, 100–101; and
    translators, 77